Praise for M.

Mark's eye for seeing things is unmatched compared to any other coach that I've ever worked with. When I was in a really bad slump in 2008, Mark came out and, in a matter of 30 minutes, my game immediately felt good enough that I believed I could win again. He is very easy to work with because of his outgoing personality and positive attitude and he makes everyone that he comes into contact with a better bowler and a better person. I am very glad to have met Mark, and he is now not only my coach but also someone that I consider a friend. Thanks for all that you have done for me!

—*Tommy Jones – 14-time PBA Tour champion*

To compare Mark's philosophy on teaching, one would have to evoke Jeet Kune Do, the philosophy of the late martial arts legend Bruce Lee. He is able to take an individual's strong points and then maximizes them to the best of the person's ability. Mark never tried to "force" a particular form or style on myself. He took what I had and worked on improving it. In just three years, Mark has taken me from a 100 average to 210 in three different leagues!

—*Richard Velazquez*

I have known Mark Baker for almost thirty years both as a professional bowler and as an acquaintance. So when I decided I needed a couple of tune up lessons, I called Mark. Mark's reputation as a coach was well known and I wanted to experience it first hand. We connected right away and I was immediately impressed with his coaching eye.

There was great chemistry between us and I immediately understood and agreed with his philosophy. Soon after that, Mark asked me to join his Camp Bakes coaching staff. Of course, I jumped at the opportunity and to this day do not regret my decision.

My first camp was an overwhelming experience. I was not only impressed with Mark's bowling knowledge and his organizational skills but most of all, his compassion and rapport with the bowlers. His communication skills and energy level are second to none and he has a wonderfully interesting way of conveying information to bowlers, regardless of their ability. He makes you feel comfortable and encouraged at the same time, but is never patronizing.

Mark Baker is one of the elite coaches in the world, he has a commanding presence when he speaks and he does so in a way that is not intimidating. He incorporates humor and a lot of personal stories into his teaching, so both students and coaches alike are motivated to be the best they can be.

—Robin Romeo – 17-time PWBA Tour champion

Mark Baker and I first met as competitors on the PBA tour in the 1980s. He was a great bowler even though he really doesn't talk much about that any more. Boy did he know how to strike.

After our touring days, we worked together at Columbia Industries, in the sales department for Track Bowling. As usual, Mark was a blast to be around. We had some great times but he had a serious passion to coach and make his mark by helping people enjoy the sport more – at all levels – so Mark took another job in sales that allowed him more freedom to stay near home and coach.

Not too long after that, I remember getting a call from Mark telling me that he was going to quit his sales job and become a full-time bowling coach. I felt if anyone could do this, it would be Mark. The rest is history. I can tell you for sure it is the best decision he made for him, his family and his passion for bowling.

What makes Mark a great coach? I feel there are multiple things that all come together to make him so good at what he does. Even though he's had a lot of success coaching Tour-level players, what impresses me most about Mark's coaching is his work with the beginner to the 180 average bowler.

He has a complete understanding of the game and how to help bowlers at all levels achieve the most they can with their abilities. I love to talk to him about his passion for helping people enjoy the sport more. He has a great attitude about who he is and how he wants to impact his students. I have had the opportunity to work with many of the same people, both before and after Mark, and the one constant is they all love him. More importantly to his students is that they all get the results they are looking for.

Mark has been a great friend for many years, I feel he is truly one of the best coaches in the world and if I were still a competitive bowler, I would absolutely seek Mark to assist me with my own game.

—*Chuck Gardner – PBA Tour Rep – Brunswick/DV8 Bowling*

I have attended Camp Bakes for the past four years. The first year I attended the camp I had a left knee that was in constant pain and in desperate need of repair. Mark saw something in me and was determined to help me improve my game. It worked. After the first camp my average improved by 10 pins. That same year, On December 6, 2008, I had my left knee replaced.

The second and third camp I worked on my timing and reading the lanes. After those two camps I won more tournaments than I had ever won in the past. My fourth camp, October 2011, was my best camp ever. I finally learned how to execute my shot with confidence and consistency. Everyone back home at the local bowling alley noticed my improvement and asked, "What happened?" As if it happened over night. I told them it was Mark Baker. It's Camp Bakes...This is the one camp where you get the full package - one-on-one coaching with the pros, classroom presentations, new equipment – fit to perfection, and a wealth of knowledge about the game of bowling.

At the writing of this, my game is the best it's ever been. I'm bowling four nights a week consistently and confidently and it's all because of the Best Bowling Coach on the planet - Mark Baker. Thanks Mark for believing in me.

—*Jennifer Thomas*

What can I say about Mark Baker and Camp Bakes? The first time I heard of Mark's bowling camp I was in a class working toward my masters and surfing online for bowling balls. I told my best friend, "We've got to go!" That was in 2006 and we have been going every year since. I went to camp to fix my swing.

Mark has a very unique way of coaching. Mark looks at your style and sees how he can tell you how you can improve it without drastically changing your style. He can tell you something very simple that would make a drastic improvement in your game. Since I have been going to camp my average has improved 10-plus pins. My consistency has improved and I have been cashing in more tournaments. The pros on his coaching staff are the best and I now consider them all my friends.

I've since taken what I learn at camp and pass it forward to the kids I coach on Saturday mornings. The main thing I trust Mark. He cares for the sport – it's in his blood. Camp Bakes is my home away from home. Camp Bakes is my heart. Thank you Mark for being an extraordinary coach.

—*Joyce R. Lawson*

Seventeen months ago, I was a PBA Regional player whose game was at a low point. I wasn't bowling tournaments and was thinking about hanging up my bowling shoes and devoting my time to golf. I knew Mark Baker from my days bowling PCB and PBA tournaments. I knew that he was a talented bowler, but it turns out that his real talent and desire was coaching amateur bowlers.

Mark was giving lessons at Surf Bowl so I decided to give him a chance to resurrect my game. He watched me bowl and then said that he could make me good if I trusted him.

Since my first lesson I have shot five 300 games, an 803 series, and set high average at my local center. I have a new attitude towards bowling. I am scheduling myself to bowl more tournaments and I have a level of confidence that I thought I would never see.

I owe all of this new talent and confidence to Mark. During each lesson, I look forward to hearing what is working with his PBA Tour players and how it will work for me.

Thanks Mark for all of your hard work, time and interest in making us all better bowlers.

—*Howard Stiles - PBA Regional Member*

THE GAME CHANGER

A simple system for improving your bowling scores

MARK BAKER

The Game Changer: A simple system for improving your bowling scores

Published by Wheatmark®
1760 East River Road, Suite 145
Tucson, Arizona 85705 U.S.A.
www.wheatmark.com

ISBN: 978-1-60494-774-8
LCCN: 2012932235

This book is dedicated to my partner, my wife Shannon,
thanks for always believing in me, I love you!

Contents

Foreword xi

1   Discovering a Coaching System That Works for All
    Bowlers. 1

2   How I Conduct a Lesson 25

3   Why Do I Miss My Target and How Do I Fix It? 51

4   Why Is My Timing Off and How Can I Fix It?. 87

5   How Can I Tell When Everything's Going Right?. 121

Acknowledgments 145

About the Author 149

Foreword
by Chris Barnes

Like many bowling fans, I first saw Mark Baker on ABC on Saturday afternoons back in the 1980s. He was a big California surfer dude that could bend it way before Beckham. He was a TV fixture and a favorite for a few really great years and then – POOF! – he was gone. A nagging back injury ended his career. I honestly didn't think much more about him until I hurt my back filming a commercial for ESPN mobile and, all of a sudden, I could barely crawl to the bathroom, let alone throw a 16-pound bowling ball. Immediately, out of seemingly nowhere, my thoughts went to Mark and to the idea that my run as a top player on the PBA Tour could be over just like that. If something that bad could happen to one of the pretty people, then why not me?

Fast-forward a few years. Now injury-free and, fortunately, still enjoying success on the pro tour, Mark calls and asks if I would be interested in being a guest coach at one of his camps (apparently, his first four choices couldn't make it). After having attended more than my fair share of camps and observing the varying theories and approaches they espoused, one thought had pretty consistently stuck out – "Am I a successful bowler because of, or in spite of, the way I play the game?" The reason this thought kept cropping up was mainly because if I were to follow the letter of the law according to most of the camps I'd ever attended, then I'd need to make some serious changes before I'd fall into the "good bowler" category. As someone who is always striving to improve and also to understand the root of my own success for the purpose of prolonging it for the greatest possible amount of time, it was highly frustrating to me that there was very little, if anything, in the way of coaching advice that was both an effective tool when teaching other players of varying skill levels and that could be applied toward helping me to improve my own game without completely tearing it apart and rebuilding it from scratch. That is, until I encountered Mark's system for the first time at his camp.

By that time, I'd been blessed to have been coached by my father, then local Topeka legend Wayne Sanders, Wichita State coach Gordon Vadakin, WSU "C" team coach Pat Henry, WSU player-coach (and one of my personal idols) Rick Steelsmith, Team USA coaches Fred Borden and Jeri Edwards, short stints with Susie Minshew and Ron Hoppe and – after I turned pro in 1998 – ball motion guru Rick Benoit. Leave it safe to say that, at this point, I thought I had left no stone unturned. Although each successive coach passed on great amounts of knowledge that I was able to synthesize and incorporate into my game, it wasn't until I met Mark and began to understand his system that I realized that there could exist a complete, open-minded philosophy of the physical game that could both explain why I'd had so much success in the past (and also what went wrong when I didn't reach my goals) and also offered explanations for how I could not only sustain that success but even improve upon it in the future. In short,

I realized for the first time that I hadn't just been a lucky stiff for all these years after all! And now, because of Mark, I could actually see the reasons why!

My first classroom session at Camp Bakes included fellow coaches Dave Husted, Joe Hutchinson, Barry Asher, Kim Terrell-Kearney and one of my best friends, John Gaines. It was quite a group of assembled knowledge to be sure. When Mark started to speak to the group of 35 (who each paid $1,000 – not included travel expenses – just to attend) I remember thinking, "This guy has some incredible passion and energy – and he seems to really believe what he's talking about." Soon, he starts talking about a measurable "timing spot" that players from Tommy Jones to Carolyn Dorin-Ballard to Dave Husted all have in common. Now he really has my attention. This is a totally new spin on things and it sounds really great but, being the skeptic, I wait and see how it applies when we get on the lanes – and if it has any application that can actually help bowlers improve.

At most of the camps I've attended or served as a coach, the typical number of bowlers who visibly improve by the end is in the 30 to 40 percent range. At the first Camp Bakes I attended, 34 out of the 35 campers made significant strides in their game in just three days (and the 35th is the typical guy that didn't come there to improve, just to be told that he is already good). Aside from the astounding success rate, perhaps more amazingly, I'd watched some of the greatest names in the sport all buy in to Mark's system and teach it effectively – if you haven't been around bowling, where everyone thinks they know it all and couldn't possibly be troubled with someone else's ideas or philosophies, this is a truly inspiring feat. In addition, for the first time, I found myself completely energized by doing a camp, rather than drained. I loved being a part of an overall plan that was making sense not only to me, but that I could

teach to a 160-average bowler as well! There was no clashing of
egos that comes when my theories are pitted against the pro/
coach next to me, because Mark's system applied not only to
what I do, but was also applicable – and, more importantly,
HELPFUL – to every single bowler I worked with over that
three-day period!

At that point, I was sure he could help anyone from the
beginner to the 220-average bowler, but could he help a tour
player? As I said, I was quite possibly the most-coached player
in bowling history, but was there something he could see that
someone else hadn't? So partway through the 2009 season I
decide to ask Mark to help me figure out why I had trouble
closing the deal on TV. I mean, that's the million dollar question
right? Well, in a short amount of time, he goes way above and
beyond and pulls out youtube videos, old ESPN Classic PBA
shows and even some rickety old VHS tapes he's collected and
shows me a common mistake I make when I really "try" on
a particular shot. By combining his first-hand experience of
throwing those shots for a living himself and the knowledge of
how to identify the good and the bad from his "spot," I make
a few small changes and the very next week I threw multiple
clutch strikes to steal a title away from Bill O'Neill (who now
is also one of Mark's clients). Then I won the next week too (on
TV mind you!) Two weeks later, I qualify third for the season-
ending U.S. Open show, where I need the 1st strike in the 10th
to beat Mike Scroggins and bowl for the title and Player of the
Year (which would have been pretty cool considering how far
out of the race I'd been just four weeks earlier).

When I step up on the approach, I can feel that old feeling
that would come on when I really "want" one, but now I know
what my tendency is and how to correct it. I execute one of the
best shots of my life, but leave a stone 8 (sometimes, bowling's
just not fair, but what are you gonna do?). I end up losing the

tournament, but now I know for certain – I may not win every show I make, but now there won't be any gifts caused by my old TV-induced nemesis any more. Since I've been with Mark, I've never been more comfortable on TV, and my results back that up. In 2011, I won four straight TV matches for the PBA World Championship title, which allowed me to join five other all-time bowling greats (Billy Hardwick, Johnny Petraglia, Mike Aulby, Pete Weber and Norm Duke) as the only players in history to win professional bowling's Triple Crown (the U.S. Open, the Tournament of Champions and the World Championship).

Like Fred Borden, Mark has the gift of an eye for motion. It doesn't take him many shots to not only see irregularities, but to identify the fixes as well. Whenever a coach has made suggestions to me regarding my game, it's always been my practice to question it. There are two reasons for this – 1) To fully grasp the idea behind the suggestion so I understand it – if I can't follow the logic, then the end result is not likely to have a very good outcome and 2) to see if the coach really knows what the heck he is talking about. Mark is the only coach I've worked with who can field a seemingly endless series of bowling "whys" and, because his system covers every element of the physical game, he can continue to respond with answers that make sense. Because of this, I believe that Mark's system is revolutionary and truly something that will change the way the sport is taught, which bodes well for the future of competitive bowling. I believe it is truly a game changer.

1

Discovering a Coaching System That Works for All Bowlers

One of the things that people love most about the sport of bowling is that anyone can do it. Whether you're big, small, tall, short, young, old, weak or strong, you can still play the sport of bowling. And because of that, there are literally almost as many bowling styles out there as there are bowlers. It seems like no two people throw the ball exactly alike and what works incredibly well for one person may not work at all for someone else. When you look into it a little more closely and begin to examine the kinds of bowlers who've had the most success over time, you might be surprised to discover pretty much the same thing. There are great tall bowlers like Mika Koivuniemi and Wes Malott and there are great short bowlers like Norm Duke and Carolyn Dorin-Ballard. There are highly successful bowlers who like to throw a big hook (Tommy Jones) and some who throw a small one (Walter Ray Williams, Jr.). Some bowlers prefer to throw it hard (Jason Couch) and some like to throw it soft (Mike Aulby). Some (like Chris Barnes) are pretty good at everything! Some great bowlers have a high backswing

(Mike Fagan) and some barely swing the ball above their waist (Dave Ferraro). But which way is right? And how do you tell which way is best for you?

Now, if you're a bowler who just wants to get better (and let's be honest, who doesn't want to get better?), how can you ever expect to sift through the mountain of bowling styles, techniques, tips, philosophies, failed experiments and great success stories and determine which way is the right way for you to bowl? Wouldn't it be nice if someone developed a logical, universal system for throwing a bowling ball that could help to improve any and every bowler and bowling style under the sun? As someone who was trying to make my living as a bowling coach, I sure thought so, and figuring out a way to do that became my goal. Through a lot of research, trial and error and with some luck, a few years back I began to figure out a very simple, uncomplicated system of analyzing the act of throwing a bowling ball that I now fully believe has the ability to help any bowler to improve their game (and, most importantly, their scores) in a very short amount of time.

The Epiphany – Discovering Some Universal Similarities Among Good Bowlers

The Timing Spot

One day, I was sitting in an empty bowling center waiting for a client who was stuck in L.A. traffic and running late for a lesson. This particular client had wanted me to help him learn to throw the ball like Tommy Jones (the 2005 PBA Player of the Year and the fastest player to reach 10 titles in PBA history) – which had become pretty much the most common request I'd been hearing from students. Of course, I'd been trying to steer people more toward throwing it like Carolyn Dorin-Ballard (the deadly-accurate USBC Hall-of-Famer), who, to me, was the benchmark for a textbook bowling game. At the time, I'd been thinking a lot about how to incorporate elements of Tommy's athletic, powerful, modern style into Carolyn's textbook game to create a unified physical game philosophy that I could teach to my students to help them improve their own games. Ideally it would combine sound, consistent fundamentals like balance, rhythm and timing with some of the flashiness and fun of the power game, namely increased rev rate, speed and momentum. For me, those things are what sports are all about – whoever can generate the most momentum with the least amount of effort and the greatest degree of control will have the best chance to win – and bowling is (contrary to the belief of some, shall we say, less-enlightened individuals) most definitely a sport!

So I sat down with my laptop and began looking for similarities in Tommy and Carolyn's games using video footage I had archived on Bowler's Map[1]. I put them side-by-side (looking at a side view of both) and began to analyze each of their games step by step. On step one, nothing matched. Step two, nothing. Step three, not even close. In step four, I began to see one similarity in that the position of their head in relation to their pivot steps[2] were pretty close, but their swings were in completely different spots. Then in their fifth and final step, when their slide foot got flat on the floor just in front of their heads, I noticed something very interesting. A phrase I'd recently heard from Randy Pedersen on the Professional Bowlers Association (PBA) telecasts on ESPN popped into my head and made me stop

---

1   Ebonite's proprietary video analysis coaching software

2   The second-to-last step in the approach, followed by the slide, in most cases.

the video at the point when "their swings were parallel to the floor." All of a sudden, both bowlers looked like carbon copies of one another! As their slide foot got flat on the approach, their swings were both parallel to the floor. When I first noticed this I thought I must have done something wrong because there was absolutely no way in the world that Tommy Jones, who throws one of the most powerful strike balls in the world, and Carolyn Dorin-Ballard, who is known for her accuracy, could possibly be in the same position at this late point in their approaches. So I ran the video again. And again. And again. It was the same every time!

Fig. 1-1

Then I took a random sampling of about 20 clients I'd filmed and viewed them from the same spot. They represented a wide assortment of styles and skill levels: from power players, to strokers[3], to in-between – bowlers who averaged anywhere from 150 to 220. None of them got there.

---

3   A stroker is a bowler who relies on accuracy more than power. Typically, strokers have lower rev rates, medium to slow ball speed and a very simple, compact delivery.

They all had issues with their consistency too – from missing their target, to inconsistent rev rate[4], to lack of speed control. All of them especially had problems keeping their balance at the finish.

At that moment, I decided I was going to conduct an experiment with my late-running client and see if I could get him to "the timing spot" during our lesson. After tweaking a few things with his footwork and timing to get him closer to the spot, he saw immediate improvement in his game – THAT SAME DAY! I was very excited and, after the lesson ended, I couldn't wait to get home to sit down with my treasure trove of past PBA telecasts on ESPN Classic to see if there were any other great bowlers whose timing matched at the same spot as Tommy and Carolyn. (Needless to say this was probably the one time in my life that I was ever thankful for L.A. traffic!)

After getting back home and plunking myself down in front of the TV to watch some classic pro bowling, what I found was nothing short of unbelievable. Almost every great contemporary bowler matched! Mark Roth, Dave Husted, Amleto Monacelli, Doug Kent, Chris Barnes, Bill O'Neill – each of them highly successful, world-class players – they all matched. Then I looked at a few of the all-time great woman bowlers like Robin Romeo, Leanne Hulsenburg (formerly Leanne Barrette), Liz Johnson and Kelly Kulick – they all matched! At about 11 pm, after five straight hours of exclaiming "THEY MATCH!!!!" (getting louder each time) with every successive example, my wife (and even my cats) started to think I was going crazy. But I knew I was on to something.

---

4 Rev rate describes the amount of rotation a bowler puts on the ball. This is measured in Revolutions Per Minute (RPM). Power players' rev rates are in the 400-600 RPM range, while strokers are below 300 RPM.

ROTH (1978)   HUSTED (1986)   MONACELLI (1990)   KENT (2000)   BARNES (2007)

O'NEILL (2011)   ROMEO (1988)   BARRETTE (1992)   JOHNSON (2000)   KULICK (2010)

Fig. 1-2

The thing that was unusual about this timing discovery was that it was almost a complete one-eighty from everything I'd ever learned about how to measure a bowler's timing. For decades, the most common way for measuring a bowler's timing was to determine when the bowler pushes the ball away at the start of his approach. Using a five-step approach as the standard, whether or not someone had late or early timing depended upon when they pushed the ball away in relation to taking their second step. If they pushed, then stepped, they were early. If the push and step came at the same time, they were "in time." If they waited to push the ball until after their second step was complete, they were considered late.

Bowlers who took more or less than five steps were measured the same way, except the steps below or above five were either subtracted or added and timing was determined based on when the ball was pushed in relation to that fourth-to-last step. So, a four-step player who pushed the ball away on his first step was said to be in time. The same with a six-step player who pushed it away at the start of his third step, and so on. Not all coaches measured timing this way, however. Some measured it based on where the ball was at the completion of the slide. If the ball was at the point of release when the slide was completed, you were in time, if it was still in your hand, you were late and if it was already off of your hand you were early. The problem with all of these methods was that they had no ability to predict whether or not a bowler would be any good. Among any sampling of good bowlers, you could find any number of them with different kinds of timing (both at the pushaway and at the release), and no one way was the obvious best way for every player. For every great player who had a late pushaway (Chris Barnes, for example) or released the ball after the slide was complete (Parker Bohn III), there was someone who pushed it early (Tommy Jones) and released it at the same moment as the slide (Mika Koivuniemi). It was very hard – if not flat impossible – to tell which way was right. Like collecting butterflies, it was very good for cataloguing and categorizing, but not so much when it came to suggesting meaningful changes to help a bowler improve. As far as I could tell, no one had ever considered measuring timing at the same spot I was now proposing to measure it, even though that spot seemed to be the only place where all great bowlers looked the same. For me, this was a truly game-changing discovery on the road to developing a universal system that could help any bowler or bowling style!

Good Direction

After discovering this new spot for measuring timing and building a mountain of Hall of Fame examples to back it up as the only truly universal timing measurement system, my next job was to identify any other similarities I could find that made good bowlers good and why.

One piece of information that came to mind right away was that lower average bowlers (in the 160 and under range) had trouble hitting their target (or, more specifically, throwing the ball along the same target path shot after shot). None of them got to the timing spot, of course, but their issues were even more fundamental in that they had a difficult time walking to the line and throwing the ball consistently. One time they would slide to the right and pull the ball across their body, missing badly left, and the next shot they'd slide to the left and spray the ball dead right of where they were aiming. Or on one shot, their swing would bounce out to the right and they would pull the ball across their body and, on the next, the swing would wrap behind their body and the ball would go dead right. Every now and then everything would come together and they would throw a perfect strike – and then they would desperately try to figure out what they did right. They'd almost always say, "That one felt so good and easy! Why can't I just do *that* every time?" I knew the answer was, "Because your footwork and swing path are inconsistent."

I had already been filming clients from the side and from the back as part of my coaching assessments during lessons, but now I began thinking about the reasons why I measured from those vantage points. What I discovered pretty quickly was that the view from the back helped me to determine how consistent the bowler's direction was. Could the bowler hit his target (both at the arrows as well as at the break point[5]) numerous times in a row? Could he throw a shot without losing his balance? Did he walk to the line relatively straight? Did the swing path of the ball follow a straight line, or did it bump from side to side like a pinball, requiring massive amounts of muscle manipulation and momentum-killing redirection? What I then realized was that good bowlers (above 180) generally have pretty good direction. For example, you don't hear many Tour

---

5   The break point is typically a spot 40-50 feet down the lane where the ball begins hooking toward the 1-3 (or 1-2 for lefties) pocket.

players say, "Man, I just can't hit what I'm looking at today!"
– and if you do hear one say that, they are usually going home
broke pretty quickly! But that kind of thing is ALL you hear
with bowlers who average less than 180, because usually their
footwork and swing paths contain flaws that make them very
difficult to consistently repeat. So, I realized that the first thing
I needed to look at when I evaluated a new client was: Does
the bowler possess footwork and a swing that promotes consistency? Over the course of this process, I did the same video
comparison with a huge sample of excellent bowlers and also
discovered a number of similarities that these bowlers had in
common. All of these similarities were related to their footwork
allowing their swing to go straight back and straight through[6]
unimpeded along the target line, in spite of their wide-ranging
diversity of styles.

Good Speed Control

I next realized that the physical game features I commonly
analyzed from the side view predominantly affected timing and
speed control. In bowling, it's not always enough to have good
direction, because if your ball speed and rev rate are inconsistent then – even if you are hitting your target – you are just as
likely to miss at the pins than if you'd missed your target. It
logically followed then, that when I looked at a bowler's game
from the side I wanted to see where his weight was distributed throughout the approach and if the shifting of the weight
was accomplished in a way that made it easy for the bowler
to repeat shots consistently with a minimum of effort. Was
the person's weight too far forward, requiring him to use his
shoulder, arm and wrist to pull the ball through at the release,

---

6 Actually, almost no one walks perfectly straight, even among the best
bowlers in history.

thereby killing the ball's momentum and creating an unnatural, hard-to-repeat delivery? Or was the person staying too far back and then lunging forward on the last step in an effort to make up for some other issue (like too quick a pushaway or steps that moved too slowly) that occurred at the start of the approach?

What I discovered again was that the great bowlers had a lot more in common at certain points in the delivery (namely, during the pivot step, the timing spot, the release point and the finish position) than one might imagine at a casual glance. Before long I began to develop the ability to identify any given bowler's root problem simply by watching a few shots and determining whether the lack of consistency was caused by direction-related issues within the footwork and swing path or whether it was caused by timing-related issues like early or late timing, a short pivot step or inconsistent spine tilt. From there, it didn't take me long to see how all of these elements were interrelated and then develop a logical system for suggesting small, incremental changes to a bowler's game that allowed him to resemble the greats in certain key positions, while maintaining their own unique style that was comfortable to them. Once I had this system in place and began using it with my clients, it allowed me to help bowlers improve their ability to throw the ball more consistently and increase their scores in a very short amount of time.

The way this worked when I saw a new client for the first time was very simple. Did the bowler have problems hitting his target? If the answer was "yes," I'd start by looking at the footwork and the swing path from the back. If the answer was "no," and the issues tended to be more a lack of consistent speed control or rev rate, I knew the problem had to be in the timing so I'd watch from the side. And once I had the key similarities represented by my growing video library of Hall of Fame-caliber bowlers in which to compare my clients, it grew easier and easier for me to help more and more bowlers to improve their consistency and reach their goals faster than ever.

My Coaching Philosophy: Improving Your Game Without Tearing You Apart

There was a young student I worked with in Canoga Park a few years back. The student was a teenager who came to me with the goal of winning a tournament in the same Southern California junior bowling club in which I grew up competing. During our first lesson, I noticed that he did some things very well, namely, he had a strong release and he was also an accomplished athlete in other sports, which meant that he had well-above-average hand-eye coordination and physical strength. His problems were mainly that his footwork was very inconsistent (his drift pattern[7] varied widely from one shot to another) and his swing was all over the place.

After our first few lessons, he began to show some marked improvement, but he was also pleased to see that I had not asked him to completely tear apart his game from the get-go. After working together a few months, his game had made such improvement that I felt it was merely a matter of time before he would reach his goal of winning one of these high-level junior tournaments. Although we used video in every lesson, it wasn't until he asked one day to see the video from his first lesson that he realized just how much his game had changed. Using a "before and after" shot of his first lesson and his most recent lesson side-by-side, he realized how much straighter he was walking, how much better his swing lined up with his

---

7 The measurement of the direction of your steps throughout your approach.

intended target line and how much his game now resembled
a top Tour player at the spot I use to measure timing (not to
mention how much better his scores were). I'll never forget his
words after watching that comparison video: "I can't believe
how much better it looks now! But I never even felt a thing
the whole time! *You changed me without ever making it feel like I
was changing!*" Yet, step-by-step, with small changes that each
led to incremental improvements in both form and score, this
young man's game had evolved from a better-than-average
league bowler to potential Tour player without even knowing
or feeling it until it had already happened. That is my philosophy of coaching: to make you better within the context of your
natural game.

How This Book Works

When I first decided it was time for me to write a book,
I wanted to be sure I could explain my system in a way that
would allow anyone to understand the keys to what makes
a good bowler, how to analyze and identify those keys and
then what changes to suggest in order to improve consistency
and increase scoring. As I mentioned at the beginning of this
book, there are almost an infinite number of ways to bowl and
I don't believe that any of them are wrong or right. It's just that
some are harder to repeat and some are easier and our goal is
to make your game as easy to repeat as possible.

The next chapter (Chapter 2) will help provide a starting
point for assessing your game and then, starting in Chapter 3
and continuing through Chapter 5, we'll answer your questions
about the physical game in great detail. In Chapter 3, you'll find
out why you miss your target (both to the right and to the left),
and what you can do to hit it more often. In Chapter 4, we'll
explain what causes you to lose control of your speed and your

rev rate and how to dial those in by improving your rhythm, timing and balance. And in Chapter 5 we'll give you some cool things to look for to determine whether or not you're throwing it the way you want to and how to fix yourself on the fly!

Along the way we'll be sprinkling an assortment of stories, anecdotes and bits of other relevant information throughout to expand upon the information presented or describe it in a different way (sometimes, the hardest part of coaching is to communicate a concept to a student who is not getting it and your job as a coach is to try and find new ways of communicating it so that the idea gets through to the student – some of the stories, footnotes and quick lessons in this book are designed to do just that). Some of these stories might explain and/or debunk some of the tips you've probably heard throughout your bowling life that I find to be either archaic, unhelpful, or just flat wrong. Some will discuss my own perspective on the greatest bowlers in the world, what makes them so great and some of the things I've worked on with them to keep them competing at the highest level. You'll also find footnotes that will either explain certain terms or concepts more in depth, highlight a person who deserves credit for a certain idea or philosophy, or even tells a story about my time on Tour or as a coach. Perhaps most importantly, we will include a case study at the conclusion of each chapter that will pull specific examples of some of my more high-profile clients employing the strategies discussed in that chapter to help improve their own games. Many of these stories are really incredible and inspirational and should help you to understand that bowlers even as successful as Chris Barnes and Tommy Jones go through periods where their bowling is less-than-perfect and how coaching and practice allowed them to return to the form that has made them each first-ballot Hall-of-Famers.

Before we close this chapter, I also want to be very clear

about what this book will NOT be. This book will not go into deep detail about lane play strategy or bowling equipment. Do I think these things are important? Do I think they've had an impact on shaping the best strategies to employ in the physical game so bowlers can get the most out of the information available? Yes and yes. But even for high-level scratch bowlers, what we will be discussing in this book (the physical game) is by far the most important piece of fundamental knowledge in building a solid bowling game. And if you do all of these things well, you can take any additional information you learn about lanes and equipment and apply them more easily because you are analyzing all of that information from a basic foundation of consistent performance and shot-making. In other words, if you know you're throwing it good, and you make what you think is a good shot and the ball doesn't do what you expect it to do, you know you need to make some kind of an adjustment right away. On the other hand, when you're not making good, consistent shots, when something goes wrong you wonder if it was you or the lane and you waste precious time trying to "throw it better" when the real solution might just be a move with your target or a ball change.[8] The solution? Throw the ball more consistently and you will make faster moves!

So, there it is. You now know what you're in for. Before we move on, I sincerely wish you the best of luck on your journey to improve your bowling. To summarize what we've learned in the space of the last several pages, let me just say that 1) I've discovered a game-changing, all-inclusive method of measuring and improving timing that applies to any of the literally thousands of unique styles out there that will help improve

---

8   At my bowling camps, John Gaines is the expert instructor on equipment. His favorite piece of advice for bowlers who insist that they're missing because they're "throwing it bad" is "Well, then throw it bad from somewhere else!"

your ability to bowl higher scores immediately through small, incremental changes, 2) it is based on facts, empirical evidence and measurable results, 3) some of the best pros in the world (Chris Barnes, Tommy Jones, Bill O'Neill, Jason Couch and many others) have used it to either reach or remain at the pinnacle of the sport of professional bowling, 4) you'll need a video camera to get the most out of it and 5) it's going to be a lot of fun – especially after you start tossing six baggers around like bags of peanuts at a baseball game! Now, as the dude at the counter says before you start bowling on league night: "Good luck and good scoring!"

The Sport Has Changed, Shouldn't Coaching Change Too?

It is true that the things I teach as a coach are often a departure from many of the things I've seen and heard being taught over the course of my competitive and, now, my coaching career. But the reason my philosophy and my methods are different isn't so much because I have a nonconformist streak (although that much is true and may be a small part of it), but more because the sport of bowling has changed so much over the last 20 years. Namely, there are three fundamental changes we've witnessed in the sport that required bowlers to modify the way that they play the game in order to have the most success. Here is a list of these changes and the impact each have had on the best ways for bowlers to attack the playing environment:

Change #1 – The Lanes Are No Longer Made of Wood

Back when I was growing up in the mid-1970's all bowling centers had wood lanes[9]. Every couple of years the center would shut down for a week or so to have the lanes resurfaced and recoated in order to smooth the playing surface and eliminate the wear and tear of hundreds of bowling balls being thrown down the lane. In the mid to late 1980's bowling centers began installing synthetic lanes, which were made of hard, nearly indestructible, urethane material. Today, it is very difficult to find a bowling center that still has the old, natural wood surface. In fact, during

---

9   Typically, the front part of the lane was made of maple (a harder wood which absorbed the wear and tear of bowling balls landing on the lane) and the back part was made of pine.

the 2010-2011 PBA Tour season, none of the bowling centers that hosted an event had a wood surface – they were all synthetic.

The difference in the two surfaces is basically that, since wood is a softer, more porous surface, there tends to be a very well-defined ball-track[10] and the oil tends to settle more quickly. This reduces carry-down[11] and allows the ball to hook earlier than it would on a synthetic lane. With synthetics, the harder surface reduces the influence of the ball track so that lane patterns tend to develop much more dependent on the lane play that takes place on that particular day. Also, since the harder, less porous surface allows the ball to have a larger area of surface contact with the lane, once the ball reaches the back end[12], the extra friction causes the ball to hook much more sharply than it does on wood[13]. Also, since the oil carries down[14] much more quickly on synthetics, adjustments must be made much faster.

---

10   The place on the lane where the majority of bowlers throw the ball. Over time, a groove is built into the lane, (usually between the 10th and 15th board) which helps dictate the place on the lane where the most mistake area develops.

11   The migration of lane oil from the front part of the lane to the back part of the lane – and oil patterns tend to run between 32 feet and 45 feet in length.

12   The dry, un-oiled part of the lane. Usually, the last 20 feet or so of the lane.

13   On synthetics, the ball path is more of a "hockey stick" shape. On wood, it is more of a "banana" shape. Hence, the greater importance on straight lines when it comes to swing and target paths.

14   When a ball is thrown, it drags the oil down the lane with it, picking up oil from the first 30-45 feet of the lane and depositing it on the last 15 feet of the lane.

2 – The Bowling Balls of Today Are Way Better

When I was bowling on Tour[15], the balls were polyester or urethane and contained small, pancake-shaped cores that weighed in the neighborhood of three ounces. Nowadays, the coverstocks[16] of balls are made of a resin material that exponentially increases the amount of surface contact on the lane, while the cores are made of as much as five pounds of high-density material that are then offset to increase the dynamic imbalance in the ball. What this does is that it creates track flare[17], which both allows a fresh part of the ball's cover to come into contact with the lane throughout the ball's journey from foul line to pins, and also changes the orientation of the weight block to encourage the ball to make a specific motion at given points (either more, less, earlier or later hook, basically).

The pros are typically masters at understanding how these options can enhance their ability to knock down pins, and they also employ the help of "ball reps"[18] to strategize

---

15   I competed on the PBA Tour from 1982-1990. I won four career PBA titles, made 28 TV appearances and led the Tour in average during the 1985 season. I was never quite THE MAN, but I sure got to bowl him enough to know what great bowling was supposed to look like!

16   The outer shell of the bowling ball.

17   The ring of oil that is left on the ball where the surface was in contact with the lane. In my day, this was usually a half-inch wide with little or no deviation. Now, the rings form a "bow-tie" shape, with as much as six inches of deviation between one ring and another.

18   Bowling ball experts employed by manufacturers to travel on the Tour for the purpose of assisting staff players. I actually worked as one for Track back in the early part of the decade, where I had the opportunity to work with the legendary Walter Ray Williams Jr. for a while.

over which ball is just right for overcoming a particular condition they are facing at the time. Of course, if you can't throw the ball in the right direction on a consistent basis, all of the technology in the world isn't going to help you much! And that's where I come in!

3 – There Is Much More Oil on Today's Lanes

The main effect of the new reactive-resin bowling balls is that they absorb a great deal more oil than the balls made back in my day. Back then, a typical lane needed just a thimble-full of oil spread across the surface for conditioning and protection. Nowadays, this amount has increased to a beaker-full, and the oil itself has been chemically altered to increase viscosity and durability. What this does is that it magnifies the difference between the front (oily) and the back (dry) part of the lane, making the ball travel even straighter through the front and making the hook on the back end seem even more pronounced. As we mentioned above, this causes conditions to "transition" much more rapidly (and more often), making your ability to stay on top of the changes even more imperative. Again, the key to reading these changes accurately however, is continuing to make good, consistent shots – because making a move off of a bad shot is often just as costly (when it comes to your results) as making a bad shot in the first place.

These changes in the playing environment have consequently made an enormous impact on the set of successful strategies good bowlers employ in their physical games. As we discussed earlier, we've seen players' timing (using my method for measuring) evolve to become later. Back in the 1950's and '60's we saw players swinging the ball down much earlier (meaning the swing was lower than parallel as the slide foot gets flat) than they do nowadays in order to get the ball onto the lane earlier, so that it would get into a roll as quickly as possible. Nowadays, getting the ball rolling too early is often counterproductive to power and, ultimately, achieving a high carry percentage[19] (although there are many situations where getting the ball to roll early is desirable, such as on difficult conditions where hitting the pocket more often is valued more than the percentage your pocket hits actually strike), as it reduces the angle that the ball breaks into the pins.

In a later chapter we will discuss the issue (or should I say, the myth) of "dropping your shoulder[20]," but for our purposes here, let's just say that this is a move that makes much more sense now in a world where it is better to project the ball further to the right to allow for it to have enough room to hook back and still hit the pocket. This is also related to the issue of "opening your hips and shoulders[21]" more toward the target, which is something we see a lot more of today than we have in the past, for the same reason. An interesting piece of information related to this topic for all of you true bowling fanatics out there is that the pros of today tend to look for "swing" in order to create "hold"[22], whereas, in my day, we tended to look for "hold" to create "swing." What I mean by this is that the pros are always looking for a spot on the lane where they can miss right ("swing" it) and still get

---

19   The percentage of strikes you throw on a pocket hit. Pros consider 80-90% good, although to watch their reactions, you'd think they expect every pocket hit to strike!

20   Allowing your throwing shoulder to drop below the level of your other shoulder.

21   Turning your hips and shoulders toward your target so that your body faces the direction you will be throwing the ball.

22   Swing is area that a bowler can miss his target to the right and still get the ball back to the pocket. Hold is the same thing, only to the left of target. (Directions are opposite for left-handers).

the ball back to the pocket, so, when they do miss left, the ball still "holds" it's line and hits the pocket. If you think about it in this way, it makes complete sense that today's pros build their games around the need to project the ball on a much more left-to-right path than pros had in the past.

The bottom line is that the sport of bowling has changed quite a bit over the last 20 years and, I'm sure it will continue to change even more over the next 20. In order to stay competitive as the sport changes it's imperative that we evolve with the times and constantly look for techniques that prove successful. That is what I've tried to do as a coach in developing my own system and I think it is a very healthy thing for you to do the same with your own game.

Case Study #1
Which Great Players Do Not Match The Timing Spot?

Even though the vast majority of great bowlers (especially Hall-of-Famers) match up to the spot I now use to measure timing, there are a few who do not. Many of the pre-1960's era players have much earlier timing (where the ball is past parallel, closer to the floor when the slide foot is flat), because these players were trying to get their balls to roll as early as possible because of the lack of hooking potential inherent in the rubber bowling balls and lacquer lane surfaces of the day. But as the equipment and technology improved and began favoring more speed and more hook, players' timing adjusted with it. In the modern era, two names that come to mind right away who don't match the timing possessed by their peers are Marshall Holman and Jason Couch (the latter of whom I actually happen to coach).

Marshall had a very unusual game, incorporating ultra-fast footwork and an extremely long slide that caused him to be very early with his timing (in the way I measure it, that is). As Marshall's slide foot got flat, his ball was about halfway between parallel and perpendicular to the floor, and he "flipped" the ball off his hand at the release point (in fact, at the peak of his follow-through the palm of his hand was completely turned toward the pins, which made him unique among pros). During the 1970's and throughout the 1980's this style worked extremely well and allowed him to dominate the Tour alongside Mark Roth, Earl Anthony and later, Pete Weber. I believe the reason Marshall was able to succeed in spite of his unusual timing was because he was one of the best athletes ever to bowl on Tour, and his leg-strength-to-body-weight ratio was off the charts (Marshall liked to run and bicycle long distances when he wasn't destroying bowling pins). This allowed him to use his pivot step and long slide (versus a longer swing arc) to generate the additional necessary speed and power that his early timing cost him.

Jason Couch is on the opposite end of the spectrum, that is, someone with extremely late timing. As Jason's slide foot gets flat his ball is still well above parallel, and he makes a violent motion at the finish, straightening his right leg and moving his head forward as he comes through the ball. While this style allowed Jason to lock up first-ballot Hall-of-Fame career stats (including an unprecedented three-peat in the prestigious PBA Tournament of Champions), it also put a lot of strain on his right knee, which gave out during the 2007-2008 PBA Tour season.

Since then, Jason's made great strides to rehab and he's modified his game to take some of the pressure off of his surgically repaired knee. I started working with Jason in the summer of 2009, specifically on the issue of keeping his head back (over his slide knee) and his hips down at the release point. After making a couple of TV appearances in the Shark Championship and the U.S. Open during his comeback season in 2009-2010, he returned to the winner's circle in 2011 at the Mark Roth Plastic Ball Championship[23].

From a coaching standpoint, my opinion is that these two freakishly talented athletes are the exception, rather than the rule, and the evidence shows that doing it the way the vast

---

23 During that telecast, you can actually hear Jason reminding himself to keep his head behind his knee.

majority of the sport's all-time greats have done it is the way
that will yield the best results for you.

Fig. 1-3

2

How I Conduct a Lesson

Probably the most common request I get from new students is to help them to increase their rev rate. That's not too surprising, since rev rate is the new buzz phrase among bowlers (especially younger males) that equates to how much power you possess. The most common misperception about rev rate is that it is generated by the strength of your release. In fact, it is much more about the optimal use of gravity by matching your footwork with your swing speed to release the ball with the greatest possible amount of controlled momentum behind it. Another common misperception about rev rate is that people also equate the amount of rev rate with how well a person throws it (i.e. the higher the rev rate, the better a person is said to throw it.)

During a lesson, what usually happens when I try to help someone to increase their rev rate is that I identify where the swing and footwork fail to work together, then suggest small changes that improve the bowler's efficiency of motion, which usually ends up increasing his rev rate as a consequence. When they see this happen though, their first reaction isn't usually "WOW! This is great!" It's more like, "WOW! Now, how can we get my rev rate even higher?!" That's usually when I invoke one of my favorite lines: "Unless you're averaging under 160, you don't need to throw it BETTER, you just need to throw your best shot MORE OFTEN."

Now let's think about this for a second. Let's say you were an alien and you landed in the parking lot of Woodland Bowl right smack dab in the middle of the 2010 U.S. Open bowling tournament. You go inside and you see all these pro bowlers throwing balls at pins and knocking them over with incredible efficiency. It is very unlikely that you'd latch on to Walter Ray Williams Jr. as the most exciting and/or platonic example of great form just by watching him. I mean, the guy has a very unique style, to say the least. But he's also the most consistent bowler when it comes to sliding in the same place and throwing the ball on the same target path seemingly *every single time*. And over the long formats used on the PBA Tour, this consistency has put Walter Ray in the top five more often than any other player in bowling history (172 TV appearances through the 2010-2011 season). Why? Because even though Walter Ray's best shot isn't nearly as impressive as Tommy Jones', Walter Ray throws his best shot more often than anyone else.

As a matter of fact, the three greatest bowlers in the history of the sport (Williams, Earl Anthony and Don Carter) all had pretty unique styles, but they all found a way to win because of their superior consistency. The reason I know so much about this is because I first went out on the PBA Tour in 1981, right at the peak of Earl Anthony's dominance. After five weeks of struggling I called my dad and said, "This Earl Anthony guy is overrated! He can barely get the five out[1]

---

1   When the ball contacts the 5-pin on a pocket hit, as opposed to deflecting so much that it does not touch the 5-pin. By the way, back then, getting the 5-pin out was not a god-given right as it is now with the superior bowling ball technology!

and he leaves more flat sevens[2] than anyone on Tour!" My dad replied simply, and correctly: "Yeah, but I've seen him on TV four of the first five weeks and here you are calling me for money again so you can stay out there." My dad was right. I had fallen into the trap of believing that being a successful bowler meant that you had to "throw it good," which was some arbitrary construct that required a certain level of power and some magically concocted essence of form that nobody could describe – but that the "experts" could supposedly identify when they saw it.

After bowling on Tour for nine seasons, competing in a few hundred Pro-Am events where I saw literally thousands of bowlers of all skill levels, and then becoming a coach and seeing thousands more, I can honestly say that I've never seen two different individuals throw the ball exactly the same way. Sure, some people have pieces of their game that are similar to another bowler, but I challenge anyone to film two bowlers, lay the video on top of one another and show that they match completely at every point in the delivery. It just doesn't exist. Yet for years, one of the most common methods of coaching was to teach bowlers a specific move (such as a pushaway move, a shoulder turn or a follow-through technique) made popular by that particular coach's "bowler du jour", even if that meant completely changing a person's game to the point where the things the person did well were utterly lost in the change. In this book, we will not be doing any of that.

That brings us to the point of this chapter, which is to describe how I assess bowlers for the purpose of helping them to improve their games. The reason this is important is closely related to the reason I decided to write this book in

---

2   A pocket hit for a left-hander, where the 7-pin is left standing after the 4-pin lays in the left gutter instead of ricocheting into the 7-pin.

the first place, which is to give you access to (and the ability to apply) the tools I've used to help so many bowlers – for the purpose of improving your game. But first we have to assess exactly what things you do well so we can build your game around them. The next step is to then isolate the things that need work and begin fixing those. It is through this process that we can begin seeing immediate improvement in your game, rather than the "stab-in-the-dark-and-hope-it-works" or the "you'll get worse before you get better" progression that never worked for me as a bowler – and still doesn't work for me now, as a coach.

Identifying What Kind of Pushaway Timing You Have

Figuring out which Hall-of-Famer you throw it like the most is one of the coolest things you'll do when it comes to evaluating your game. As we discussed in the opening chapter, I believe there are three different categories of pushaway timing and that every bowler falls into one distinct category. Each of these categories are represented by Hall-of-Fame-caliber bowlers. The bowlers I like to use are Chris Barnes, Carolyn Dorin-Ballard and Tommy Jones (although sometimes, if I know a student likes another player – say Mike Fagan – of whom I happen to have video available, I will swap them out). To avoid confusion, the kind of timing I am referring to here is old-school pushaway timing, because, as we saw in our first chapter, all of these bowlers look the same at the timing spot I prefer to measure, which is – let's all say it in unison now: "When the swing is parallel to the approach and the slide foot gets flat on the floor!"

My First and Last Golf Lesson

One of the most embarrassing moments in my life (and this is saying something considering an incident I was probably most known for back in my touring days[3]) was when I once tried to take a golf lesson. Now, I am an OK golfer for someone who only plays about twice a year (I usually shoot in the high 80's to low 90's) and this one time, a few weeks before the date my old man and I were scheduled to play our annual round, I decided to take a lesson to see if I could improve enough to finally beat him for once (he's a few-times-a-week player who shoots in the mid-80's).

I showed up at the driving range for the lesson (although they actually try to make you sign up – and pay for – a series of lessons up front) and hit a few practice shots before the pro got there. I was hitting it OK. After the pro showed up, he took a look at my swing and asked me to try something. For the next five minutes I hit nothing but shanks. And I'm not talking little shanks, I'm talking about line drives straight right going about 100 miles per hour. At about the ten-minute mark I look over to the guy for some advice and he says, "Hold on for a second. I'll be right back."

When he comes back he's got the entire staff of instructors with him and he's saying, "You gotta see this guy! He's hitting the worst shanks I've ever seen!" The other guys are

---

3   I won my first PBA title in Miami and, on that week's show, Bo Burton told the story on air of how I had split my pants during the competition. Wouldn't have been a big deal except for my penchant for not wearing underwear. The next week, there was a big box of skivvies that folks from around the country had sent in for the PBA to give to me. Carmen Salvino and Dick Weber had also arranged for a giant pair of underwear with the words "Moon Over Miami" emblazoned on it to be hung in the locker room.

fascinated by this (and enjoying it just a little too much for my taste) and one of them asks me if I can get my shoulders turned just a little bit more. I reply, "No, three quarters is as far as I can turn since I had back surgery." The guy replies, "Well, then I guess you're never going to be a very good golfer. And part of that is you have to be willing to get worse before you can expect to get any better." After about another five minutes of shanking and the entire facility now laughing at me, my ego starts to kick in a bit.

"So, you guys are pros, huh?" I ask.

"That's right." They all say.

"Well, how come you're not in Akron right now playing the PGA tour stop?"

"Well, we're not tour pros, we're teaching pros."

"That's funny, because in my sport when you say you're a pro that means you can make a living at it by playing."

They pretty much left me alone after that, but that experience did do a lot to shape the way I treat people when I'm giving lessons. It made me promise never to laugh at or make fun of people who are coming to me for help. Heck, even in my own bowling career there was once a time when I wasn't very good at it and, luckily, people found it in the hearts to help me. So I get it. You're just trying to get better at something and you want some help. To me, treating people the right way and seeing them improve is probably the biggest reason why I enjoy coaching more than anything I've ever done in my life.

Engineers Are the Hardest Lessons

There seems to be a very large preponderance of engineers who like to bowl in the Southern California area. Early on in my career, they also happened to be the category of people with whom I had the hardest time communicating. The reason engineers were so difficult for me to coach is because they tend to be empiricists and, as such, always require a logical, numbers-driven explanation when it comes to asking them to make a change. For someone who was grasping for his own method and philosophy as a coach, however, this was probably the best thing for me because it forced me to think about developing a system that allowed me to suggest logical, arguable changes that were based on fact, rather than regurgitate some other coaches' philosophy and try to make it fit.

Here is how a typical lesson would go with one of these technically-minded individuals:

ME: Well, I think it might help if you tried pushing the ball a little earlier in your approach.

ENGINEER: Why is that?

ME: Well, why don't we just try it and see what happens?

ENGINEER: What if I just walked faster instead?

ME: I don't know. I guess that might work too, but I'd rather see you just push it earlier because that's an easier fix.

ENGINEER: But how is pushing it earlier going to make me better?

ME: I'm not sure it will but I want to see if it does.

ENGINEER: I guess we can try it, but I don't see how it's going to help.

Notice how wishy-washy I was in that exchange? How could I ever have expected that any person (let alone a person who comes at life from such a logical, skeptical point of view) would embrace a change with any hopes for success with such a weak-willed "expert" leading them? But now that I have my own system in place (and utter confidence in its effectiveness), here is how these exchanges typically go:

ME: I want you to push the ball a little earlier in your approach.

ENGINEER: Why is that?

ME: So that when you get to the spot where your slide foot is flat, instead of your swing being above your head, it's parallel to the floor.

ENGINEER: Why is that?

ME: Because if I can get you in that timing spot, then your balance will be better at the release point, you'll stop falling out of every shot and your direction and speed control will be more consistent.

ENGINEER: Now that makes sense. I can do that.

The other thing that really helped in my interactions with engineers was the use of video. The reason was, before I had video proof, whenever I tried to convince one of these engineers to try something, they would inevitably question the reasoning behind it. Without video, I was forced to convert something that the bowler was feeling into my own understanding of mechanics (which, before I developed my system was incomplete), then describe the changes I believed the bowler needed to incorporate in terms of feel. But they wanted a mechanical explanation for the change as evidence! And when I was forced to describe the thing (often poorly) in mechanics, they could sense my lack of confidence and could easily poke holes in my reasoning. Then, even if they were nice enough to try my suggestion, if there was even the slightest appearance that the changes were not leading to rapid improvement, they were gone.

But with the combination of video and my system in place, instead of regurgitating mechanical theory and trying to force it down someone's throat, I can sit the person down next to me and show him exactly what I mean and why it will work for him. One of the most satisfying experiences I ever have as a coach now is when one of these students, after initially sounding skeptical of my verbal explanation, watches video and gets the light-bulb-over-the-head look and says, "Oh, so *that's* what you meant!" That, my friend, is pure coaching nirvana.

Chris Barnes Timing (Late Pushaway)

"Chris Barnes Timing" is the rarest of the three categories of timing I teach, and it is also the only one that I might suggest a person to change (although this is usually a last resort) because it is the most difficult to repeat on a consistent basis (which is also one of the reasons – in addition to being a workaholic, obsessive, hypercompetitive, freak of nature – why Chris Barnes practices so much). The identifying features of this type of timing are a late pushaway. Chris pushes it at the end of his second step in a five-step delivery, (which is more than half a step later than is classically recommended), followed by a quick swing and shorter-than-average third and fourth steps. The trick to bowling this way and still getting into good position in the spot I use to measure timing (swing parallel/slide foot flat – just checking!) are those quick third and fourth steps.

The problem with this style (and the thing I work on with Chris the most) is if the middle steps start to get too short, the head tends to get too far in front of the legs, which then requires a lunge in the slide step to bring the weight back to the core. More often than not, this results in a too-steep swing, making it difficult to maintain balance at the finish and, consequently, consistent direction, speed and rev rate. The bowlers who are able to pull this kind of timing off best are usually excellent athletes in good physical condition. If a bowler I'm working with possesses this kind of timing but lacks the physical gifts to pull it off consistently, I may try and convince him to get the ball started a little earlier so that their game resembles this next category of timing.

Fig. 2-1

Carolyn Dorin-Ballard Timing (Textbook Pushaway)

As we mentioned in the last chapter, Hall-of-Famer Carolyn Dorin-Ballard is a perfect example of what has long been taught as the "correct" approach to timing. Carolyn pushes the ball away precisely when her second step commences (she takes five steps) and then keeps a steady, even pace throughout the remainder of her steps.

The main advantage to this kind of timing is consistency, mostly because the swing and the footwork are never that far out of synch. It is also the best kind of timing for bowlers who are further along in years and/or lack the physical strength or athletic ability to overcome the kinds of lags in swing speed or footwork featured in the other two categories of timing. The consequence of this (there's always a consequence when it comes to moving bodies and objects – I'm not saying it, Sir Isaac Newton is) is that bowlers with this kind of timing tend to have a lower rev rate than other bowlers and must rely on accuracy and consistency to knock down the pins. Of course, if you look at most of the all-time greatest professional title winners in bowling history, most of them (Earl Anthony, Norm Duke, Walter Ray Williams, Jr., Brian Voss, Parker Bohn III, Carolyn Dorin-Ballard, Robin Romeo, Lisa Wagner and many, many others) had this type of timing, so it's obviously pretty effective if you do it the right way.

Fig. 2-2

Tommy Jones Timing

These days, with the advent of the power game, supersonic bowling balls and high-friction lane surfaces, "Tommy Jones Timing" is the most common type of timing that bowlers either want or already have. This kind of timing starts with an early pushaway (before the second step begins in a five-step approach) and then forces the player to "catch up" to the ball throughout the rest of the approach. This process of catching up is accomplished by increasing the speed of your steps and/ or the length of your backswing (which gives your feet time to catch up and your body a chance to redistribute its weight back into the lower half in preparation for the delivery).

The main advantages to this type of timing are increased potential for achieving higher rev rate, ball speed and loft[4], all of which are useful tools in today's modern bowling environment. Of course, there are drawbacks as well, most notably when it comes to issues of matching the swing with footwork at the timing spot (which we also saw with Chris Barnes Timing). When it comes to Tommy's game in particular, the problem he runs into most is that when he tries to get a little extra "oomph" on the ball (either with rev rate or speed), he'll lengthen his swing so it gets out of position (on the late side) at the timing spot. (We'll discuss this problem and it's fix fully in the Case Study for this chapter). For the same reason we saw with Chris Barnes Timing, the best candidates for Tommy Jones Timing also tend to be younger, stronger and fitter, although, sometimes (as we'll see in this chapter's Case Study) it can also help people who are smaller in stature to increase their ability to gain speed, power and accuracy.

Once you identify what kind of timing you have, you can begin to pinpoint the specific fixes (which we will learn all about soon) that will correspond to your specific game. This will eliminate entire subsets of possible fixes that simply do not apply to bowlers with your specific category of timing, consequently reducing the number of possibilities, hence making the process of improving your game simpler – which is what this book is all about. After identifying the kind of timing you

---

4   Throwing the ball over the front part of the lane (also called the "heads"), which many pros will do when the oil in that part of the lane is either scarce or becomes depleted due to heavy lane play.

have, then your next step is to begin determining your most common misses, which will direct you still more specifically to an even smaller subset of possible fixes – making the process of improving your game even simpler yet.

Fig. 2-3

Identifying Your Most Common Misses

In spite of appearances (and what you might find on a typical afternoon of open play at your local center), there are really only four misses in the sport of bowling. Assuming you know where you're trying to throw it, then this knowledge will allow you to determine not only when and where you miss but, hopefully, after understanding what you've learned so far and then incorporating what you're about to learn in the rest of this book – why you missed there and how to fix it. But first, here's what the four misses are and the most common reasons for them.

NOTE: The directions of the misses described below are specific to right-handers throwing a conventional, right-to-left hook. For left-handers, simply reverse the direction of the miss.

Miss Right, Throw It Too Fast

Let's start off with the "miss right, throw it too fast" miss because it is usually the easiest to diagnose (and fix). Missing right and throwing it hard is a pretty bad miss to have as your most common miss because it gives you virtually no chance to strike[5]. If you think about the bowling lane as a ramp designed to funnel errant shots back to the pins (more specifically the pocket[6]) – which typical league conditions help you to do if you throw a hook – then throwing it too hard and too far up the ramp is a sure way to miss (obviously to the right) where you're trying to hit at the pins.

Now, the overwhelmingly predominant cause of this miss is because the bowler is walking toward his target (that is, drifting to the right), and aimed way too far to the right with his body position. The way you can measure this using video is by freezing the bowler at the top of the swing and drawing a line from the ball, through the arm, and out onto the lane. What you always see is that this line is quite a bit further to the right than where the bowler claims to be aiming. To complicate matters further, the bowler's rightward drift usually includes a step to the right in the pivot step[7], which blocks the path of the armswing and causes the ball to be naturally projected even further to the right.

----

5   As opposed to missing right and throwing it too slow and/or missing left and throwing it too hard, which both give you at least a reasonable chance of striking.

6   The pocket is a two-inch wide area located between the 1 and 3 pins for a righthander. If the ball is sitting in contact with the lane anywhere between the left half of the 16th board to the right half of the 18th board when it hits the pins, then your ball is in the pocket.

7   The second-to-last step in the approach.

DIRECTION OF
SWING PATH

INTENDED
TARGET LINE

Fig 2-4

Usually, this miss can be fixed simply by getting the bowler to walk a straighter line to the target and also by keeping that pivot step from going to the right. While this doesn't necessarily change the path of the swing (sometimes, that's a different issue as in the case of a lateral pushaway move), it does have the effect of refocusing the player's target line into a straighter orientation. What will help though, is getting the pivot step going further left, which will clear more space for the swing to fall directly down the intended target line, which will help eliminate that miss more often than not. By fixing these two things, your new misses are most likely to fall under the category of these next two we're about to describe.

Miss Right, Throw It Too Soft and Miss Left, Throw It Too Soft

These two misses are the two that are the most closely related – interchangeable really. They happen when the bowler's swing, footwork and/or balance are out of position and some form of arm or hand manipulation is required in the last step in order to throw the ball on line. These two misses exist in varying degrees in the games of the greenest amateurs all the way up to the high-average league or scratch bowler and are characterized by the following symptoms:

- You tend to bowl better the 1st game of league and then struggle toward the end as the lanes start to hook more.
- You have trouble generating adequate ball speed.
- Your rev rate is lower than you'd like it to be.
- You tend to drift right.
- You have trouble keeping your balance.
- You can't stay behind the ball, and tend to "top it".

While it is fairly obvious to see where these problems occur when watching a beginner (usually, it is just a simple issue with the direction of the footwork and swing path), at the level of the good league bowler the differences are much more subtle, but just as easy to recognize through the use of video. Predominantly they are due to early timing at the timing spot I measure, which we will discuss in detail in Chapter 4.

Miss Left, Throw It Too Hard

This is what I like to call the "Pro Miss" because it's the most common miss that you'll see the pros and high average bowlers make. You can often even isolate the miss to shots that are really important, such as when a bowler needs a strike to win a match, to roll a 300 game or to make a cut into the next round of a tournament.

What happens physically to cause this miss is similar to a golfer "peeking" early after a swing (or a putt) to see where the ball is going. Former PBA Player of the Year David Ozio calls this miss the "Failure to finish the shot" miss because what happens is, instead of holding the finish position (the spine tilt[8], the knee bend, the head position and the follow through), the bowler comes "up and out[9]," which is followed by a late attempt to "save" the shot by turning the wrist and hand more abruptly during the release. This causes a reduction in rev rate and an increase in tilt[10]and speed, causing the ball to either hook later or less overall than the bowler intends it to. Usually this miss leads to a light hit[11] and some form of a 2-pin combination leave, or in many cases, the dreaded 2-8-10 split, which is nearly as impossible to convert as a 7-10 or a 4-6-7-10 split.

The good news is that all of these misses are treatable and

---

8   The angle of the spine in relation to the approach – there will be *much* more on this later.

9   Up and out is characterized by the spine angle straightening, the hips and shoulders coming up through the release and a loss of balance and a step out toward the throwing side of the body.

10   The degree of angle that the ball's axis points in relation to the lane. More tilt means the ball will hook later.

11   A ball that hits the 1-3 just right of the pocket, hitting the headpin too thin for it to be driven into the 2-pin.

the rest of this book is dedicated to showing you exactly why they happen and exactly what you need to do to eliminate them. But first, in order to do that, it is of utmost importance that you identify when they happen and set out to find what is causing them to wreak havoc on your ability to make your best shot more often and, most importantly, on keeping you from bowling your best possible scores.

Bad Direction Versus Bad Timing

One more way to hone in on exactly what part of your game needs work is to classify your misses as either directional or timing-related. A directional miss is characterized by an inability to hit your target or to throw the ball along a consistent target path that is virtually parallel to the path along which you intend your ball to travel. The main complaint you hear from bowlers who have direction issues is, "I can't hit my target more than twice in a row! I throw one shot left, then the next one right – I have no idea where the ball's going!" Typically, these misses are related to footwork and swing path issues, which I analyze using video shot from directly behind your throwing shoulder.

Timing problems also can cause direction issues (although usually, these direction issues are more subtle than the ones caused by poor footwork and swing path), but more often they take the form of inconsistent speed control and balance. Bowlers who truly have timing issues tend to tell me, "I'm hitting my target consistently, but I'm still having trouble hitting the pocket" or "I can hit the pocket, but my ball is hitting weak and leaving a lot of corner pins." The good news here is that if this is truly your only problem then – more than likely – you already have decent footwork and a straight swing path and all you need to work on now is perfecting your timing (which

You're Only As Good As Your Misses

There is a famous quote, often attributed to golfing great Nick Faldo, that goes, "You are only as good as your worst misses."[12] What he meant by that is virtually identical to what I mean when I say, "Don't try to make your best shot better, try to make your best shot *more often*." At the highest levels of sports like golf and bowling, the top pros make plenty of great shots. And their best shots are really, really great. But what determines success at the pro level is minimizing the damage when you don't throw your best shot. When you miss, what kinds of things are you leaving? Do you leave flat-10s or 4-pins or 2-pins? Or are you leaving big-fours[13] and 2-8-10s and washouts[14]? The bowler who minimizes the damage on the bad shots is the one who usually ends up emerging victorious in the long run on the PBA Tour. The moral: Make your misses better!

---

12 I am sensing that a few of you out there are beginning to say, "Hey, for someone who says he hates golf so much, you sure do use a lot of golf examples." My answer: "I never said I hated golf – just golf instructors!"

13 The 4-6-7-10 split.

14 A split where the headpin is left standing.

means you're already a fairly decent bowler!). I evaluate issues of timing using video shot from the side, and I look at a number of things that we'll discuss in detail throughout the remainder of the book.

Becoming a Champion at Your Level

The first thing I do when I'm with a new student is that I ask a lot of questions (actually, asking a lot of questions is something I always do with all of my students, because that's the only way to find out what problems there are to fix). One of the most important things I ask is for you to define the ultimate goal you want to achieve through our time together – which I like to call, "Becoming a Champion at your level."

At my bowling camps, I employ the services of several of my fellow bowling peers, who each teach my system to the students who patronize us. The common link between the entire coaching staff is that we were all champions at the highest level of the sport. I won four PBA titles in my nine-year pro career, Barry Asher is a 10-time PBA champion, Dave Husted won 15 career titles (including three U.S. Opens), Tommy Jones was the fastest player to reach 10 career PBA wins (and now has 13 and counting, including two majors), Jason Couch is a 16-time champion and the first player to win three consecutive Tournament of Champions, Chris Barnes also has 13 titles and is just the sixth man in bowling history to win the Triple Crown[15], Joe Hutchinson has four PBA wins, John Gaines was one of the top amateur bowlers in the world in the 1990's and is now one of the foremost experts on lane conditions and bowling ball

---

15   The Triple Crown consists of the PBA World Championship, the Tournament of Champions and the U.S. Open. Chris also has two 2nd-place finishes in the USBC Masters, which, if he can win, will make him just the third player in history to complete bowling's Grand Slam.

layouts, Kim Terrell is a two-time Women's U.S. Open champ, Doug Kent is a former PBA Player of the Year with 10 career PBA titles including four majors, Lynda Barnes is a two-time winner of the USBC Queens and a 10-time member of Team USA, Kendra Gaines holds two career PWBA titles and is a four-time member of Team USA and Robin Romeo was also a former U.S. Open champ and the LPBT Player of the Year in 1989. We are all champions in our sport at the world-class level and one of the first things we like to identify with all of our bowlers who attend camp is to find out how each of them are hoping to become champions – at their own level.

Do you want to become the anchor bowler on your scratch league team? Do you want to shoot your first 300 game? Do you badly want to beat those two obnoxious guys in your Thursday night trios league? Do you want to win a PBA Regional title? These are the clear, write-them-down-on-your-bulletin-board kinds of goals that most bowlers want to attain when they seek out coaching help, whether that help comes in the form of the services of a professional coach like myself, an internet or magazine article, or a book like this one. But these goals are also related when it comes to improving your bowling, because they each boil down to increasing the number of times that you can make your best shot in a given period of competition. Obviously the higher you set your goals, the more often you're going to need to make that best shot to reach them. If you're a 160 bowler who wants to get to 180, then making two more of your best shots per game will get you there. If you're looking to get to 200, then you'll need to make your best shot even more often than that. And if you're Chris Barnes, who is looking to win every single bowling event he enters against the absolute best bowlers in the world, then your goal may be to make that best shot every single time you throw the ball. For most of us mere mortals this is unattainable but Chris actually believes he should get there and he's willing to put in as much time as it takes to do it – which is precisely what's made him the best and is what inspires me to go the extra mile to help him get there!

Chapter Summary

So now that you know all about my unique method for measuring timing and also how I evaluate my students' bowling games, it's time for us to move on to the really good stuff, which is, namely, the nuts and bolts of techniques and fixes that will allow you to perfect the most important aspect of becoming a good bowler – your physical game. The rest of the book will focus on the different pieces of the physical game, going in chronological order from the stance all the way through the finish position. As I mentioned before, there are many more aspects of the physical game that are shared by the world's best bowlers other than just the timing spot we've discussed so far, and we'll go through each of them for the purpose of helping you build a more consistent game that is unique to your preferred style of bowling.

But before we do that, let's take a moment to briefly summarize the ground we've covered so far:

- The traditional methods of measuring timing didn't work for me as a coach because there was always way too much variation among Hall of Fame-caliber bowlers.
- I discovered a way of measuring timing that is universal – that nearly every Hall of Fame-caliber bowler fits in. The best part is, as bowlers get closer to fitting this mold – which they can do regardless of their style – their games tend to improve rapidly.
- There are three categories of timing (represented by three Hall-of-Famers) and every bowler fits into one of them.

- I've had no luck with golf instructors – or the term "You're going to get worse before you get better." Either as a bowler or as a coach.
- If you want to improve, you must first identify what kind of timing you have, then identify your most common misses.
- I evaluate direction issues from behind and timing issues from the side.
- Set a goal that, when you reach it, will make you a champion at your level.

I think that just about sums it up. It may take you some time to incorporate what you are about to read into a system that allows you to pinpoint mistakes (either by feel or through the use of video), as quickly as I might be able to identify them myself. As my best friend Dave Husted says, "You can identify the problems fastest because you're the one who does the most lessons." What he means is that I do it for a living – I see it every day. I've been trained to do this through years of practice but, using the information in this book as a foundation, I know that mistakes will become more and more simple for you to identify and the corresponding fixes just as obvious. Above all, remember that my goal as a coach is to change your game in a way that makes it feel like you're not changing it at all, but in the meantime, your rhythm and timing are better, your balance is improved, you're suddenly generating more momentum than you've ever felt before and your scores are reaching levels you've only dreamed of. If you can get there, then I've done my job as a coach, which is the most rewarding thing a person can achieve in my line of work.

Case Study #2
Tommy Jones and the Old Man

One day I got a call from Ebonite Brand Manager Ed Gallagher asking me if I was available to fly out to Buffalo to have a look at Tommy Jones' game. It was still pretty early along in my coaching career and, even though I now had my own system in which I had total confidence, I was still pretty nervous to accept the invite, considering Tommy had won 10 PBA Tour titles the previous four years and was two years removed from winning the PBA Player of the Year award. I didn't want to be known as "the guy who screwed up Tommy Jones", but then again, I'd worked with him before (I even had video footage of him when he was bowling his best) and now I had this system in place that used his game as one of the cornerstones, so I sucked it up and caught the next redeye.

After I arrived at the bowling center and watched Tommy throw a few shots, I could see that – on a fairly easy league condition – when Tommy got the ball to the right it never hooked back and when he squared up[16] it hooked high (sound familiar anyone?). The fix seemed pretty obvious to me after watching video and analyzing the results within the context of my system. But before I could sit down with Tommy, an old man who was bowling a few lanes away came over and said to Tommy, "You know, when I was young and cocky like you I had a high backswing too! But now that I've cut it

---

16   A fancy term for playing a more direct line to the pocket.

down, look at my score!" He pointed to the computer monitor hanging over his lane, and the guy had the first seven strikes of the game. But we also noticed that there were little "NT" notations next to six of the seven strikes, meaning that the guy was bowling no-tap[17] and had only thrown one "real" strike all game. Tommy's face turned about as red as the old Track Critical Mass Code Red bowling ball and it took every ounce of his self control not to knock the guy out. The rest of us couldn't control ourselves and we were literally rolling on the floor laughing.

Once the hubbub died down, Tommy and I had a look at the video and noticed that his timing was extremely late, which was causing his swing to get steep and eliminating his flat spot so that he had no time at the bottom to rotate his hand through the ball like he normally does. After making a few changes to his footwork, shortening the length of his swing and getting his hips to stay level through the release, Tommy got back to the timing spot and started throwing the ball like his old self again.

TOMMY'S NORMAL (GREAT) TIMING   TOMMY DURING SLUMP

Fig. 2-5

---

17 A variation of the game where you receive a strike for getting nine pins (or less, in some cases) on your first ball.

Two weeks later Tommy was on the show again and won another PBA Tour title soon after. He's continued to be one of the best players on Tour ever since but, every now and then, we'll work on the same things we worked on that night in Buffalo to fine tune his game so that Tommy is clicking on all cylinders (heck, the old man might even be impressed!). After seeing the instant results I'd achieved with Tommy, Chris Barnes, with whom I'd never before worked, asked, "Hey! Do you think you might have 20 minutes to look at my game?" "Sure," I said, thinking, "Great, now I'll have a chance to screw up the guy who's been the best bowler in the world for the past decade!" Fortunately for me, that whole situation worked out pretty well too!

3

Why Do I Miss My Target and How Do I Fix It?

One thing I like to do at the local level to try and help as many bowlers as possible is to run low-cost weekend clinics at my home bowling center[1]. Since it is inexpensive to come out ($10 per person, which includes the cost of bowling), I always see quite a few beginners and other lower-average bowlers who are hoping to hear a tip or two that might help them score a little better in their leagues. What I also notice with these bowlers is that they almost always have an extremely hard time hitting the headpin (let alone the pocket) consistently. These folks will miss the headpin right, then miss it left and then maybe hit it once or twice before going through the same set of misses over and over again throughout the course of the night[2]. They tend to have just as much trouble making their spares, which hurts their scores even further, not to mention the frustration

---

1   PBA Tour host center Fountain Bowl.

2   We call this "Army Bowling" – as in a drill sergeant barking out "left, right, left, right" while his platoon marches.

it causes them. The goal when I work with these bowlers then, is just to get them hitting the headpin consistently and making a few more of their spares. But how do I do that? And what exactly is it that causes these bowlers to have so much trouble hitting the headpin on a consistent basis? The simple answer is that I start by assessing these bowlers' games from behind to diagnose why they have such a hard time throwing the ball with consistent direction. And it is always an issue that has something to do with the bowler's footwork and swing path, which work together to create the most fundamental element of any bowler's physical game.

But beginners aren't the only kinds of bowlers who have trouble with consistent direction. A lot of intermediate bowlers (in the 150-200 average range) struggle with this problem as well and, usually, straightening out those issues gets them to the next level. Even some advanced bowlers occasionally have problems with direction – typically 220-plus average league bowlers who struggle when they are forced to play deeper inside or on tougher, "sport" conditions like the ones you see in PBA competition or USBC-sanctioned Sport leagues. After reading this chapter, you should understand what causes these issues, and what you can do to fix them quickly and get on to the business of improving your consistency and your scores!

Gauging a Bowler's Consistency by Watching from Behind

Since bowling is a target game where the ultimate object is to knock down as many pins as possible, it seems to make sense that you'd want to be able to hit your target as much as you can to give yourself the best chance of knocking down a lot of pins. But your target is more than just a single point that you're trying to hit somewhere on the lane[3]. Actually, my philosophy is that it is much less important to "hit your target" than it is to develop a game that promotes "consistent direction." I'll explain.

Let's say you throw three shots. One of them hits the pocket for a strike, one goes through the nose[4] for a 4-6 split and the last misses the pocket light and leaves a 2-8-10. At the arrows, let's say each shot hit the same target (say, over the 10th board[5]). Let's also not confuse the issue and assume that the bowler used the same bowling ball each time and that the oil on the lane did not move between shots (this happens in the real world very quickly by the way). Bottom line, the conditions were exactly the same for all three shots. How is it possible that the ball could go three different places at the pins when the bowler hit the same target at the arrows every time? Well, one way for this to happen is, on the shot that struck, the bowler did exactly what he was trying to do. But on the 2-8-10 shot, the ball could have missed right at the pins even though it went over the intended target at the arrows *if the ball were released from left of* the shot that struck. That could happen if the bowler

---

3 Most good bowlers target at the arrows, which are 16 feet away. A lot of beginners target at the pins, which are 60 feet away. Believe me, it's a lot easier to hit something 16 feet away than it is to hit something 60 feet away – just ask PBA Hall-of-Famer Steve Cook who also used to be a competitive archer!

4 When the ball hits the headpin right in the center.

5 A lane is 41 inches wide and is composed of 39 1-inch wide boards. The 10th board is the one that is ten boards from the edge of the gutter on the side you throw from. Boards are counted from right to left for right-handers and left-to-right for lefthanders, meaning that a left-hander playing the 10th board from the left gutter is the same as a right-hander playing the 10th board from the right gutter. For a right-hander, playing the 10th board from the left gutter would mean that he was playing 30, which is a pretty common target for right-handers to play on the PBA Tour after the lanes have gone through several games of competition!

drifted further left than he had on the strike, which means the ball started left of the "target line"[6], crossed the target line at the arrows and then projected right of the target line at the break point and, ultimately, at the pins. The same would be true of the shot that went high for a 4-6, except in that case, the bowler drifted right, causing the ball to start right of the target line and then veer left of it beyond the arrows.

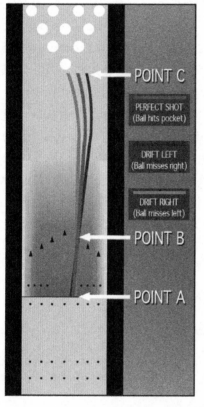

Another way for a bowler to struggle with consistent direction is for his swing path not to match up with his target line. Let's say a bowler hits his target and strikes on his first shot. For some reason on his next shot he pulls his backswing more to the inside of his body, causing him to miss right of target. He then tries to compensate by bouncing the swing out away from his body, causing him to miss left of target. On these two errant shots, even though the bowler's drift pattern was consistent and the ball was thrown from exactly the same release point, because the swing path was heading in different directions, the ball missed either to the right or to the left.

Fig 3.1

Complicating matters is that most bowlers can feel when

---

6   A line that traces the ball's intended path from the foul line all the way to the point at which the ball starts to hook – otherwise known as the "break point" – usually between 35 and 45 feet down the lane.

something is going wrong with their balance or their swing, which usually causes them to try and correct for the problem at the release point. When this happens, if the bowler's swing is wrapped too far behind his back at the top (making it look like the ball is sure to go right of the intended target line), at the last possible second he'll lunge forward with his head and throwing shoulder and pull the ball back in the other direction, causing it to miss left! The only way to diagnose what happened in these cases – and, most importantly, find the point in the delivery where the footwork or the swing put the bowler in a position that made it difficult to throw the ball with consistent direction – is to view the bowler from the back. Sometimes, the problem occurs as early as the stance (which is a very easy fix), sometimes it happens at the start of the approach (like during the pushaway) and sometimes it happens more toward the end (say, in the pivot step, which is the most common place I find problems that affect direction). Whatever the case, to improve your ability to achieve consistent direction we need to find and correct whatever problems we might discover – and the only way to do that is through close observation from behind.

What Is Consistent Direction?

What exactly is consistent direction, though, and why is it better than just being able to hit your target at the arrows? Time for a simple little geometry experiment! Let's say we have two bowlers: One who hits his target at the arrows every time and another who misses his target at the arrows quite a bit. Both bowlers play a slight hook, both have trouble drifting the same number of boards shot after shot, but only the second bowler never allows his drift to alter his swing path from the intended target line. After watching just a few shots, most people would assume that our first subject is the better bowler but, if you watch them each throw 100 shots, what becomes painfully obvious is that even though the second bowler misses his target at the arrows a lot more, he misses it at the pins a lot less. Why? Because when this bowler drifts left, he's missing left the same amount *at all three points* along the intended target path[7]! When he drifts right, the same is true. When our first bowler drifts left, sure, he's hitting his target at the arrows, but

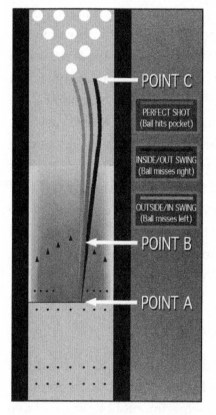

because he's started the ball further left, it means it will be a much bigger miss at the pins (to the right)[8]. So, do you still think hitting your target at the arrows is the most important thing in bowling? Sure it helps, but only if your footwork and swing path are allowing you to throw the ball with consistent direction!

Now, getting back to my reasons for assessing a bowler's footwork and swing path from behind. A couple of things to note: First, when I set up from behind to watch a bowler, the vantage point I prefer is slightly outside the throwing

Fig 3.2

7   If he is trying to hit 10 at the arrows with a lay-down of 15 and a break point of 5, then his one-board miss left will put him at 16 at the lay-down, 11 at the arrows and 6 at the break point.

8   When this guy hits 16 at the lay-down and 10 at the arrows, his miss at the break point will be 2 or more boards (depending on how much angle he is playing – the more angle the greater the miss!) right of 5 at the break point. I hope there're a lot of very dry boards to the right to help you get the ball back to the pocket!

shoulder (just right of the shoulder for a right-hander and just left for a left-hander) and from the level of the bowler's head. I also like to be able to see all of the steps in the footwork, so I prefer not to see the camera "zoom in" as the bowler makes his way to the foul line. I'll explain the reasons for this method in more detail in a bit, but for now, just understand that it has to do with measuring the path of the ball in the swing as well as the direction and length of each of the steps.

What Came First: The Footwork or the Swing?

As I said a few pages back, I believe the most important aspect of bowling fundamentals is the way your footwork and your swing work together to allow you to make your best shot as consistently as possible. And in my system, I tend to focus on the footwork first because I believe it sets the foundation for the swing. What I mean by this is, while there may be any number of ways to fix a bowler's inconsistencies (no matter what those problems happen to be), in the thousands of lessons I've given over the course of my coaching career I've very rarely changed a bowler's swing to improve his footwork. So that means in every other successful instance I've done it the other way around and changed the footwork to improve the swing. Why has this worked so well? Because good footwork allows the ball to swing freely and unimpeded, ultimately leading to an improvement in power, consistency and score – all while reducing the amount of effort required to throw the ball.

What Is Good Footwork?

I define footwork in bowling as the pattern your steps take from your stance to your finish position at the foul line. The first thing to note about footwork is that, in my experience, the quality of a bowler's footwork is directly proportional to the quality of his overall game. Exactly what I define as good footwork I will explain in step-by-step detail shortly, but for the time being, let's just say that, in general, it is relatively straight from start to finish[9], well-balanced, well-paced (meaning there are no abrupt starts, stops or lengthy pauses) and matches well with the bowler's swing path and rhythm – in other words, it complements the direction and the speed of the swing!

How Good Footwork Creates a Consistent Swing Path

Even though I believe that the footwork is the more important component in the equation that determines consistent direction, the swing is where any weaknesses or inconsistencies with your footwork are likely to show. In that respect, it is ultimately your swing (even if the swing's direction is determined mostly by your footwork) that will determine your accuracy and your ability to throw good, consistent shots. More specifically, it is the *path* of your swing that will determine how simple your delivery is to repeat – and what you will find is that the bowlers who possess the straightest, most relaxed swings – swings that stay in line with their shoulder and fall directly under the head – tend not only to have the most consistent direction but also have the greatest capacity for generating power in the form of speed and rev rate.

Now I don't have a degree from Caltech but I'm pretty sure that if you were to design a bowling ball ramp, the best way to design it so that your ball goes as fast (and as accurately) as

---

9   This is different than finishing in the same place you start. For example, you might start your approach on 20 and finish there, but if you've drifted 15 boards left or right in order to get there, your footwork isn't likely to be very consistent.

possible would be to build it high and straight. A ramp that starts six feet off the ground with no twists and turns is going to project the ball faster and straighter than a ramp that is just four feet off the ground and curves left at one point and right at another. The same is true with a bowler's swing path. From behind, I measure the swing at four distinct points in order to track exactly where your swing loses momentum and causes you trouble in controlling the ball's direction.

Measuring the Swing at Four Points

Through the process of analyzing thousands of bowlers' swings, I've determined four key measuring spots that serve as great indicators of the consistency of your swing path. These points are: 1) during the stance, 2) at the bottom of the swing as the ball is coming back, 3) at the top of the swing and 4) at the bottom again as the ball is coming through. In predicting consistency, the best-case scenario is that the bowler has the ball either in front of, directly below, or covering the head (depending on the point in the delivery) throughout the entire swing. While it is definitely better for your likelihood of achieving consistency if the ball matches at all four spots in the swing path, the importance in having the ball "match the spots" increases as the swing progresses. What I mean by this is that it is more important to match the ideal positions at the peak of the swing and at the bottom coming through than it is during the stance and at the bottom going back. Of course, the better the position of the ball in the stance and at the bottom of the backswing, the easier it will be to get the ball into those best possible positions later in the delivery, thus enhancing your ability to make good, consistent shots. But probably the best way to describe my measuring system is to take you through a series of photos to show the spots I measure and what kinds of things I like to see and what kinds of things are likely to cause inconsistency.

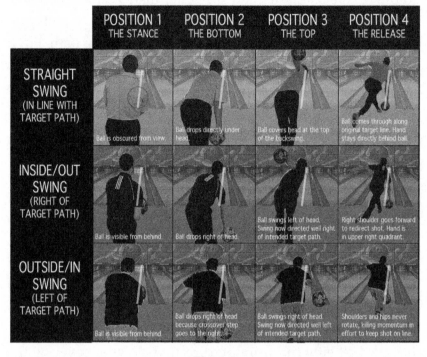

	POSITION 1 THE STANCE	POSITION 2 THE BOTTOM	POSITION 3 THE TOP	POSITION 4 THE RELEASE
STRAIGHT SWING (IN LINE WITH TARGET PATH)	Ball is obscured from view.	Ball drops directly under head.	Ball covers head at the top of the backswing.	Ball comes through along original target line. Hand stays directly behind ball.
INSIDE/OUT SWING (RIGHT OF TARGET PATH)	Ball is visible from behind.	Ball drops right of head.	Ball swings left of head. Swing now directed well right of intended target path.	Right shoulder goes forward to redirect shot. Hand is in upper right quadrant.
OUTSIDE/IN SWING (LEFT OF TARGET PATH)	Ball is visible from behind.	Ball drops right of head because crossover step goes to the right.	Ball swings right of head. Swing now directed well left of intended target path.	Shoulders and hips never rotate, killing momentum in effort to keep shot on line.

Fig. 3-3

This series of photos dramatically illustrates what I look for when I measure a bowler's swing, both from the standpoint of what it looks like when it's done in a way that promotes power and good direction versus a way that makes it very difficult to achieve those things. From here, the challenge is to pinpoint what changes need to be made (usually in the footwork, as I mentioned before) in order to promote a more consistent, repeatable swing path. The good news is that these are usually very simple changes and the place I like to start (even before looking at your footwork) is your stance and pushaway.

"Don't Drop Your Shoulder!" Actually, Do!

When I was developing my own bowling game in the late '70's and early '80's, one of the most common pieces of advice I heard was, "Don't drop your shoulder!" What the person always meant by this was that I needed to make more of an effort to keep my right shoulder at the same level as my left shoulder through the delivery. I would even see pros doing things to help them accomplish this – like George Pappas – who used to jerk his right shoulder up several times during his stance as a reminder to keep it level. The problem for me was that I never really noticed anyone who kept their shoulders level (even Pappas) at the release, so I just kind of forgot about it and would basically ignore the advice whenever it came across my path.

It wasn't until I became a coach and started to have to think about the logic of these kinds of things that I really ever gave the issue much thought once again. I always knew in the back of my mind that the "Don't drop your shoulders" thing was a little bit fishy, but I never exactly knew why or what effect dropping your shoulder had on your ability to deliver a bowling ball with consistent efficiency. Then one day, the accessories manufacturer Vise Grips released a poster that featured all of their PBA Tour and regional staff players. The poster utilized frontal views of these players at the release point, just as the ball was about to come off of their hands. Every last one of them was dropping his or her shoulder! Obviously, all of the bowlers on the poster were highly skilled and highly successful – and represented a wide range of styles – and they all happened to drop their shoulders. As you may have noticed by now, I tend to enjoy discovering little coincidences and/or patterns such as this, and I immediately concluded that dropping your shoulder must actually be a *good* thing to do if you want to become a successful bowler! It would be a few years later before I would discover exactly why dropping your shoulder is a good thing (because it helps get the ball under your head during the release, which is the last key measuring spot in the swing path) and share the info with the world in my lessons and, now, right here in this book.

I've also figured out that keeping your shoulders level (like you would if you happened to follow the "don't drop your shoulder" tip) is a sure way to pull the ball left of target – which worked OK back in the days of rubber bowling balls that barely hooked at all (hence the likely origin of the tip in the first place) – but doesn't work well at all in today's modern bowling environment that features high-friction lane surfaces and bowling balls.

What keeping your shoulders level also does is that it forces your hand and wrist into a weak position (the upper right quadrant of the ball) at the release point. The reason is because your shoulders and hips actually work in unison because they are connected, so the distance from one to the other cannot change. That means when your right hip drops down during the pivot step to clear the way for the swing, your right shoulder drops with it allowing the ball to be thrown along the intended target line. In other words, you *have* to drop your shoulder if you want the ball to do this consistently! Therefore, if you want to be a really good bowler, don't listen to the "Don't drop your shoulder" myth for one more second and keep doing what you're doing – that is, keep dropping that shoulder!

"SHOULDERS SQUARE" LINE

BILL'S SHOULDER LINE

BALL RELEASED DIRECTLY
UNDER THE HEAD (IDEAL!)

Fig 3-4

The Stance and the Pushaway

Since the stance and the pushaway are such basic pieces of the physical game, bowlers often overlook them because they naturally sound less interesting than the release or your rev rate. And because they are so fundamental and happen so early in the delivery, after a bowler throws the ball, all he usually remembers is how the delivery felt when in it came off his hand during the release. But a lot of times, a bad delivery can be tracked directly back to the stance, or to a pushaway move that is difficult to repeat. For example, a stance or a pushaway that requires a lot of strength and effort can put either the footwork or the swing path (and usually, if one goes astray, the other will follow too) out of position later in the delivery, making it very hard to maintain consistent direction.

It's no coincidence that the most important feature of the stance and the pushaway that is shared by the vast majority of pros is that they tend to be very relaxed and very easy to repeat. With the stance, you'll see that most of the best bowlers look almost identical and we'll outline each of those defining features and why they are successful in contributing to a more consistent physical game. On the other hand, you'll find that there is a huge amount of variation in the pushaways of any sampling of good bowlers (even among Hall of Fame-caliber bowlers), but that upon its completion (when the ball is at the bottom of the swing heading on its way up into the backswing), nearly every last one of them get the ball into about the same place (under the head) – which promotes a simpler, straighter swing and solid balance throughout the approach. After we have a look at these features in detail, the contrast between some of the common moves that contribute to both consistency and inconsistency – and what steps you can take to make your game more consistent – should become second nature.

The Stance

When you go to a driving range and see golfers of all different skill levels hitting range balls, you'll typically find that the ones who are hitting it the best tend to have the simplest, most relaxed stances. On the other hand, the ones with their legs wide open or their feet too far apart or their hands way in front of the ball or their shoulders tilted unnaturally from front to back are the ones hitting balls all over the place (sometimes turning the range into a bona-fide hard-hat zone). The same is true in bowling – although unlike my experience at the driving range, I've never quite seen a bowler throw it so wildly that I've feared for my personal safety!

Just as we saw when I compared the timing spots of really good bowlers, you'll also notice that good bowlers tend to look very similar in their stance. This list of similarities generally includes:

- They hold the ball in a place where it cannot be seen from behind, when the observer is standing directly behind the player's throwing shoulder.
- Their weight is balanced and the throwing arm is not bearing the entire weight of the bowling ball.
- Their knees are slightly flexed.
- Their shoulders tilt slightly down toward the throwing side.
- Their head leans slightly toward the throwing shoulder.

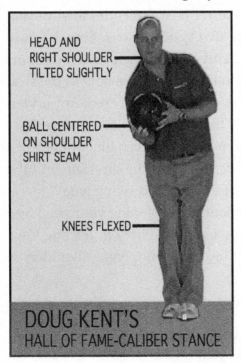

HEAD AND
RIGHT SHOULDER
TILTED SLIGHTLY

BALL CENTERED
ON SHOULDER
SHIRT SEAM

KNEES FLEXED

DOUG KENT'S
HALL OF FAME-CALIBER STANCE

Fig 3-5

Is it a coincidence that virtually every bowler in the Hall of Fame looks like this in the stance? Not a chance, so let's talk for a moment about the benefits of doing it this way. First off, the part about not seeing the ball from behind is something we mentioned in our section on measuring the swing. The reason why placing the ball in this position in your stance promotes consistency has to do with starting off the swing path in the simplest possible way. If the way to achieve a straight swing is to place the ball under the head at the bottom of the swing, then cover the head at the top of the backswing and then to release it under the head at the release point, doesn't it make sense that you'd want to hold the ball in a similar spot[10] during the pushaway? Of course! Why? Because it's just simpler that way! To make the point even further, let's say you're a lefty and you hold the ball out to the left during your stance so I can see it from behind. If you want to get the ball into a swing path that matches your intended target line, then your first move to get the ball there will have to be a lateral move to the right. This is not impossible to do[11] but it is *very hard to repeat*! So, why not just cut out the complexity and make it a straight shot right into the pushaway?

Next, what is the significance of balancing the weight of the ball so the throwing arm doesn't bear the entire load during the stance? I think there are two good reasons. First, because it reduces tension – and when you're participating in a sport that inherently causes tension by virtue of the kind of physical activity and mental strain it requires you to perform under, adding more tension is likely to hinder your performance. And second, adding tension is something that can hinder the ball's motion into the swing, which can affect the direction and the consistency of your balance, footwork and swing path[12].

Now let's talk for a moment about leaning your head and shoulders toward your throwing side. First off, leaning your head toward the direction you are leaning your shoulders is

---

10 The place I really like to see the ball rest in the stance is centered on the shoulder seam of your shirt.

11 In fact, future Hall-of-Famer Patrick Allen moves the ball laterally in his pushaway even though his starting position hides the ball from behind – but he's the only notable exception!

12 It can also affect your timing, which we'll discuss in Chapter 4.

actually just the way your body is built. (Try leaning your shoulders to the right while keeping your head straight – it's pretty darn uncomfortable unless you slept wrong the night before and physically can't hold your head straight without pinching a nerve). The other thing that leaning toward your throwing arm does is it serves as a precursor to dropping your throwing shoulder slightly as the ball comes through, which promotes releasing the ball directly under your head. Again, if you're going to end up in that position at the finish, doesn't it make sense to at least somewhat resemble that position at the start? As you can see, each of these features of the stance minimize the amount of effort required to get your bowling ball into the four key positions which promote a swing path that maximizes power and consistent direction.

The Pushaway

The pushaway is really the first piece of the physical game where there is actual movement of the bowling ball involved. The (sometimes) confusing part about this topic, though, is that if you compare any decent sampling of Hall of Famers, there are almost as many pushaway techniques as there are bowlers. In fact, it may be the worst indicator in predicting whether or not a bowler is (or will be) any good. When it comes to pushaways, there's the "over-the-bar" method, the "hinge," the "drop it on the foot," the "place it on the table," the "push-in, drop-out," the "hold-down, push-up" and many more that I'm not even mentioning here. Students of the game can no doubt cite any number of Hall-of-Fame-caliber bowlers who have utilized any one of these techniques with great success in their careers, but the one thing I've noticed about all of them is that the best players tend to have pushaways that are very simple and very repeatable and get the ball into the swing with a minimum amount of effort, tension and, most importantly, no lateral movement!

This last point is key, especially at the pro level, where the goal is to repeat shots for as long as possible as the pressure to win continues to mount[13]. But it is no less true at other levels of the sport, where your own personal goals (bowling your first 200 game, your first 300 game or your first 600, 700 or 800 series) are sources of self-induced pressure that mount with each successive strike you throw. Your ability to perform by repeating your best shot more often will determine whether you reach those goals, and your chances of accomplishing them increase when the first move you make in your delivery – the pushaway – gives you the best possible chance of achieving consistency.

Let's see if you can guess the place I like to start when I look at the pushaway. If you didn't say, "Check for lateral movement," there's a good chance you may have been skipping around these last few pages. But to reiterate, the reason I check for that first is because lateral movement in the pushaway simply increases the chances that the ball will sway out of position in the swing path and require some later manipulation in order to get the ball back on line. For example, let's say we have a right-handed bowler who starts the ball off in a nice position in the stance but pushes the ball right in the pushaway. In this case the weight of the ball will almost certainly pull his second step to the right, which then causes his swing to go further right to get around his right leg. From there, the ball comes too far inside at the top, creating a swing path that, unless redirected at the bottom, will project the ball well right of the intended

---

13   In a typical PBA Tour event, first there are qualifying rounds to determine the match-play finalists, then match-play rounds to determine the TV finalists, then the TV show which is seen by several hundred thousand households (sometimes, even more than a million) on ESPN every Sunday during the tour season.

target line. The only two places the ball can go from here are either dead right (if his pivot step comes inside and the swing goes straight through unimpeded), or any number of places depending upon the success of the strenuous arm/hand/wrist manipulation that is sure to happen at the bottom of the swing if the pivot step goes right, impeding the swing path.

Using an opposite example, let's again say that the bowler starts off his stance in a good position, but then pushes the ball left, back toward the center of his body. From there, the ball bounces out (meaning it ends up right of the head at the bottom of the swing) and once it's in that position it can go any number of ways. If it stays out to the right and ends up right of the head at the top of the swing, hopefully there is a heck of a lot of oil in the middle part of the lane because the only place that ball is going is left. If the bowler redirects the ball to get it covering the head and then swings it straight through on the downswing and the release, it could be a good shot (albeit with less speed and rotation than someone with a straight, "free" swing). If he gets it inside of his head, then he's stuck in our proverbial "no man's land" and it's anyone's guess as to where the shot might go. As you can see, whichever way the pushaway goes, there are a lot more things that can go wrong when you don't push it straight than can go right, so why stack the deck against yourself in the first place? Your goal with the pushaway then, should be to get the ball from its starting point in the stance to as close to under your head as possible as the ball goes back into the swing.

How Does the Footwork Work?

So now that we understand the importance of the swing path and the things that can cause problems with consistent direction, let's move on to examine what good footwork looks

like, step-by-step, and how it ultimately promotes a consistent, powerful swing path. For me, fundamentally sound
footwork consists of two key steps that aid in preserving
the unimpeded direction of the swing along the four points
we measure, and those steps are: the crossover step and the
pivot step. These two steps are surrounded by a collection
of steps that keep the swing and the bowler's momentum
moving forward at a pace that is natural and comfortable –
culminating in a controlled, balanced finishing step – usually
a slide, but sometimes not, as in the case of bowlers who like
to "plant" at the foul line.

The Crossover Step

The first key step in the footwork is the step I like to call
"the crossover step." In a five-step approach this is the second
step[14] (or the first in a four-step approach) and what I like to
see in the crossover step is for it to be placed directly in front
of the other foot, but no further. Why? Because this gives your
swing room to come down on a straight path (under your
head), while keeping your shoulders slightly open and parallel
to the direction that your hips are pointing. But we also don't
want to see that step cross over too much because then you
would have to open your hips in order to get the ball back into
your swing, which would cause it to come in too far behind
your head. From there, the only way to get your ball back on
line is to rotate your shoulders violently at the release. This is
not a very easy series of moves to repeat, I can assure you. The
point? Allow that step to cross over in front of your opposite

---

14   The two most successful exceptions to this rule are Leanne Barrette-
Hulsenberg and Ryan Shafer, who both cross over with their *left* foot
(Leanne's second step in a four-step approach, Ryan's third in a five-step).

foot and the ball will swing straight under your head while you walk by it – putting you in great position to swing the ball back relaxed and unimpeded!

Fig 3-6

The Pivot Step

The next key step in your approach is the pivot step, which is always completed with the same foot that makes the cross-over step. Again, it is best for this step to "cross over" as well to clear space for your swing to come through on its way down to the release. If it doesn't and your pivot step goes to the right, your swing will be forced to re-route (to avoid the hip and leg), which is then followed by some awkward arm/wrist/ hand manipulation at the release point and the dreaded loss of balance at the finish. Even if you are strong enough to pull this off occasionally, over time you're sure to struggle with your direction more than bowlers whose pivot steps cross over. On top of that, the wing of the Hall of Fame made up of bowlers whose pivot steps go right is currently empty.

What about when the pivot step goes too far to the left – in other words, crosses over too much? This is a very rare exception, but when it does happen, it usually forces the next step (the slide) to naturally go left, which then forces the ball to come left with it. It is extremely unlikely that you'd be able to keep your balance if you did that, because it would require a huge shift in your weight, (very quickly from right to left) from the time the ball started on its way down to the time you released it. If you happen to bowl this way, hopefully you only bowl on lanes where there is a ton of oil and lots of hold area[15], because the only direction you're going to be able to throw the ball is to the left. If, on the other hand, you do happen to slide back to the right, then the constant crossing of your steps is sure to wreak havoc with your swing path, leading to a multitude of issues like a lack of speed, rev rate and an inability to play the inside line very well. But mostly, all of that lateral movement requires so much realignment and redirection that it makes it extremely hard for your body to repeat good, consistent shots!

Now that we've seen what happens when the pivot step goes too far to the right or the left, how about if it goes directly under the head? Bingo! Now you have the best chance of all to make better shots more consistently. There are two main reasons why this is the case, starting with the fact that a

---

15   The area inside of your intended target path (left for righties, right for lefties) where you can miss and still hit the pocket. Usually, only oil patterns with very large volume ratios (at least 5:1, but probably even higher) would allow you to get away with this.

pivot step that comes inside your head (almost directly under it), allows the swing to pass by the leg underneath your head, which is exactly where you want it for maximum power and consistency. The other reason you want your pivot step in this position is that it allows your weight to be distributed evenly, balanced on top of your pivot foot before going into your slide. As we saw in our prior two examples, uneven weight distribution between the right and left sides of your body forces you to use quite a bit more muscle for the purpose of retaining balance than if the weight were more evenly distributed. And again, the less muscle manipulation your footwork requires you to make, the more consistent a bowler you are likely to be!

Fig 3-7

The Other Steps

Before we move on to look at the final step (the slide step),
let's take a moment to note a few things about the other steps
that comprise your footwork. Obviously, since any sampling
of bowlers are likely to exhibit huge variations in timing, there
can be a lot of variation on how the other steps might look in
terms of their length, direction and pacing. I tend not to spend
too much time on these steps during lessons, but when I do,
it is usually to suggest some change that will either help the
bowler to improve his ability to generate momentum, or to
better set up the position of the swing path via the cross-over,
the pivot or the slide steps.

The first possible step[16] would be step one in a five-step
approach, which is taken prior to the crossover step. A lot of
bowlers use this step to set up the timing in the case of a slow
(or late) pushaway, which sometimes helps to keep the bowler's
center of gravity lower and further back. Some bowlers use it
to generate early momentum although, in reality, momentum
is really best created by the swinging of the bowling ball. There
honestly is not much to say about this step except that it is
best to keep it simple (we'll talk about this in detail in our next
chapter on timing, but a long, complicated step tends to burn
up more energy, which it is best to save for the release) and
as straight as possible since, ideally, our crossover step will
follow and can then be placed directly in front of it more easily.

The step after the crossover step is actually the third step
in a five-step approach, which gets the player from the bottom
of the swing to the top. The length and speed of this step is
predicated on your category of timing: bowlers with Tommy

16	I say "possible" because in a four-step approach this step does not exist.

Jones timing will usually make this step quicker because the swing is already on its way to the top, while a bowler with Chris Barnes timing will make it slower (to allow the ball more time to reach the peak of the backswing). Bowlers with Carolyn Dorin-Ballard timing will be somewhere in between the two. As for direction, much like we recommended with our first step, it's best to keep this one as straight as possible in order to simplify the work required to place the pivot step directly in front of this step and, more importantly, under your head to balance your weight evenly from side to side. Other than that, there is a tremendous amount of flexibility in these steps that you really have to evaluate on a case-by-case basis. But when it comes to achieving consistent direction, the typical fixes tend to be straightening the direction of a "stray" step in order to set up the crossover or pivot steps in a way that allows the swing path to get into the best possible position at the top and the bottom of the swing.

The Slide Step

Last but not least, we have the slide step. As I mentioned earlier, this last step usually culminates with a slide, but not always. In fact, some excellent contemporary pro bowlers do not slide and have still enjoyed very good success on Tour[17]. So, if sliding is not the most important thing when it comes to what makes a good final step, what is? To put it simply, the answer is, "good balance." Of course, there are very specific ways to achieve good balance on the final step, but the best and most consistent is for the step to end up just slightly to the left

---

17   Dave Ferraro is probably the best of the "no-slide" bowlers in history. He bowled on Tour at about the same time I did (the mid-80's through the mid '90's) and had a stellar Hall of Fame career, making it on the "50 Greatest Players in PBA History" list that was announced by the PBA back in 2008.

of your head, so your weight is completely balanced on the leg. The way top pros accomplish that is by sliding (or planting) on the very same board as the pivot step. So, if your pivot step is on the 25th board, then your slide should also be on the 25th board[18]. If your pivot is on 15, then your slide should be on 15 as well. You get the point. What this does is that it allows your weight to shift seamlessly from one leg to the other as the ball is firing through along the intended target line.

Fig 3-8

So what happens if the final step goes left or right of this? Although I think you can guess by now, a step that finishes

---

18   I like to measure which board you're sliding or standing on by the location of the middle of the foot. Some people like to use the inside edge of the foot, but when you're measuring the position of both feet – as we are when we measure the pivot step and the slide – it's easier to go by the middle.

right (for a right-hander) will impede the swing path (making it go right of the intended target line) and require a swing/release manipulation that will adversely affect your speed, rev rate and ability to effectively play left-to-right (i.e. the inside angle). A final step that goes left will shift the weight abruptly to the left, forcing the bowler's swing to go left with the weight of the body – again, pray for lots of oil in the middle of the lane to keep the ball from heading to the Brooklyn side if your last step goes this way! So remember, center your slide step on the same board as your pivot step and you will put yourself in the best possible position for power and consistent direction!

Drifting

From what we've discussed in this chapter up until now, you might think that all I teach my students is to walk dead straight. That's not true and, in fact, I've worked with dozens of good bowlers who drift that I've never even thought about asking to change. Now, that's not to say that I wouldn't prefer the bowler to walk straighter (because I think that makes it easier to consistently repeat the same shot over and over), but I also think that as long as your footwork allows you to swing the ball along the swing path unimpeded, then your game – and your ability to make good, consistent shots – is in good shape. What I will say, however, is that if you do drift, that you are much more likely to have a good, consistent swing path if you drift away from your target (left for a right-hander) than toward it. Why is that? Because as we've spent quite a bit of time illustrating, any step toward your throwing arm is likely to impede the swing path, requiring some kind of shoulder/arm/hand/wrist manipulation or redirection and reducing the likelihood that you'll be able to make good, consistent shots.

Now, it is possible for a bowler to drift toward the target

from start to finish, without either the crossover step or the pivot step going in the direction of the swing. But the only way for this to happen is for the other steps to go back toward the target more than those other two steps go away from it. As an example, let's say you're a right-handed bowler and you start your approach (let's say it's a five-step approach) on the 20th board. By the time you throw the ball, you're sliding on the 15th board, meaning you had a net drift of five boards to the right. Now if your crossover step goes three boards to the left, and your pivot step also goes three boards left, then the other steps, collectively, must have gone a total of 11 boards to the right (11 boards right – 6 boards left = 5 boards of net drift to the right). While this is not physically impossible to do, it is very difficult to repeat, especially compared with the relative simplicity of walking straighter – just ask anyone who's ever been pulled over and asked to complete a field sobriety test!

On the other hand, a bowler who drifts away from his target is naturally more likely to possess an unimpeded swing path, because the overall direction of his drift makes it more likely that his crossover and pivot steps are going in the "right" direction (that is, out of the way of the swing). Is it possible for a bowler to drift left with one (or even both) of the two key steps going in the opposite direction, thereby blocking the swing path? Yes – and in those cases, those steps would be something I'd pick out for the bowler to work on changing – but it is not very common. In fact, if you want numbers, what I like to see is for your drift pattern to be somewhere between seven boards left to three boards right. If you're in that range, then you're off to a good start!

Playing The Inside Line

One of the most common categories of students I work with is the high average league bowler who struggles when he's forced to play inside. When these bowlers come to me it is always the same story, "Well, I average 230 in my league at home, but whenever I go to a tournament and the shot[19] is inside, I struggle to break 200." After hearing that, I watch them throw a few shots and, inevitably, I find that it is always the same reason for their struggle. Their pivot steps always go right!

We've seen the effect that failing to place your pivot step under your head causes, but at the upper levels of the sport, the biggest problem is that it prevents you from consistently projecting the ball on an inside-out target line when that is the only place the lane allows you to play in order to maximize your score. And in scratch tournaments designed for high-average bowlers this is – if not always the case – very, very often what you are required to do in order to compete.

So how do I help these bowlers fix the problem? Usually I show them what another scratch player (one who is success-ful at playing inside) does in their pivot step and then try to get the student to accomplish the same thing in theirs. If they are able to successfully accomplish the change, they usually not only see an improvement in their ability to play the inside line, but also an improvement in their overall accuracy, con-

---

19   The "shot" is the part of a particular lane (or group of lanes) where a majority of bowlers prefer to play in order to maximize score. Usually in tournaments, the leaders are all playing in a similar part of the lane to one another and it is very rare to see a player win by playing a different part of the lane than everyone else. Inciden-tally, Walter Ray Williams Jr. and Earl Anthony (the two all-time leaders in career PBA wins) are/were the best at pulling this off!

sistency and power. If they can't or won't make the change, then they have pretty much reached their peak when it comes to bowling achievement, because without a pivot step that crosses over, you will never be able to beat the better bowlers on those kinds of tournament conditions. Especially when those bowlers all have pivot steps that match "my way" – or should I say, "the Hall of Fame's way?"

Chapter Summary

Before we move on to our next chapter, let's review what we've learned here:

- Lower average bowlers typically have issues with consistent direction and I diagnose those issues by watching from behind.
- "Consistent direction" is more important than "hitting your target."
- The Footwork and the Swing Path are the two most important (and inter-related) pieces of a bowler's physical game.
- Footwork is the most important factor (even more important than the swing) in determining a bowler's shot-making consistency.
- Most Hall of Fame bowlers look very similar in their stance: they tend to be relaxed, leaning slightly to their throwing side with the ball obscured from view from behind, resting just to the side of the head.
- The Pushaway is the least reliable indicator of determining how good a bowler a person is – but the best pushaways are the ones that limit lateral movement.

- Good footwork always consists of crossover steps just prior to the pushaway and then during the pivot step, culminating in a well-balanced slide that comes in underneath the head.
- It is better to drift away from your target than toward it.
- Bowlers with better footwork can play the inside line much more effectively and are also more powerful, accurate and consistent in playing all angles than bowlers with less solid footwork.

Now that you've completed this chapter, you should understand how your footwork and swing path work together to determine your ability to throw a bowling ball with consistent direction. If you do happen to possess the solid fundamentals I've described here, then congratulations, you are probably a better bowler than most! However, if you are a decent bowler but are still struggling to reach your own personal goals, then this next chapter is for you. That's because when I work with a bowler who wants to get better but is still having trouble making that bowling ball do exactly what he wants it to do, then there must be some kind of an issue with rhythm, timing or balance – and that, my friends, is what we will be looking at next!

Case Study #3
Why Chris Barnes Is a Perennial Bowlers Journal International First-Team All-American

In 2011 Chris Barnes was voted to the Bowlers Journal International All-American First Team[20] for the twelfth time in thirteen seasons on the PBA Tour. This may not sound like too big a deal until you consider that, since the publication was founded in 1915, only two bowlers have made it onto the first team that many times: Earl Anthony and Walter Ray Williams, Jr. – guys who are generally considered the two greatest bowlers of all time. Chris, aside from being considered by his peers as the best bowler in the world for more than a decade, also has to be the most inquisitive person I've ever met in my life. He's also probably had the most exposure to world-class coaching of any bowler ever.

Chris grew up in Topeka, Kansas and, after showing some early promise as a teenager, went on to Gordon Vadakin's legendary collegiate program at Wichita State University. At WSU Chris was coached by Pat Henry (who he still calls the "most influential" coach of his career) and then by Rick Steelsmith, who was arguably the greatest collegiate bowler in history. Meanwhile, he was a perennial Team USA fixture under top coaches like Fred Borden and Jeri Edwards. In 1998, he went out on the PBA Tour where he worked with John Jowdy, Rick

---

20 Every year this highly respected industry magazine publishes its picks of three teams of the five best male and female players in the world.

Benoit, Del Ballard Jr. and many others. And now, after all that, he's with me. After working my camp in Henderson, Nevada and then seeing what I'd been able to do to help Tommy Jones when he was suffering from the worst slump of his career, Chris wanted to see if there was any part of my system that could possibly help his game. I passed his de facto interview process when I was able to answer a seemingly never-ending multitude of questions and he decided I was the guy for him. The funny thing about Chris was that he really never completely understood why he was so successful (which he mentioned in detail in his great foreword), and when I introduced him to my system, it was the first time someone explained to him why he had some of the best fundamentals in the history of the sport.

Looking at Chris' footwork from behind, his first step is perfectly straight and requires pretty much no effort. His second step (his cross-over) is to the left and directly in front of his first, almost as if he's walking a tightrope. From there, his swing drops directly under his head and he takes his third step, which is, again, straight ahead of his second. His fourth step (his pivot) again crosses under his head and goes directly in front of his third, clearing space for the ball to drop straight down the line in preparation for the release. His slide commences and concludes directly in the shadow of his pivot step (in fact, on the exact same board) and he finishes in perfect balance with all of his weight resting comfortably on his left leg. His net drift? Exactly zero boards, which makes him and Barry Asher the only two players I know of who do not drift at all throughout their approach.

So what effect does this have on his swing? If we were to look at a shot of Chris directly from behind and then draw a line that represents Chris' intended angle of play at the start of his approach, you'll notice that throughout his entire delivery, his swing path never leaves the line. In the stance, the ball is in front of him, just right of his head. At the bottom of the swing the ball is directly under his head, with his arm aligned with the original line we drew. At the top of the swing, the ball has come straight up along the line and is now covering his head. As he reaches the release point the ball is again directly under his head and his arm is still perfectly mirroring the original line we drew at the start of his approach! That, ladies and gentleman, is about as perfect as it can be done, and is also the reason I rarely ever need to watch Chris' game from behind. It is also the real reason why it is probably not a good idea to bet against Mr. Barnes when it comes to bowling success over any extended period of time – he's just too darn consistent!

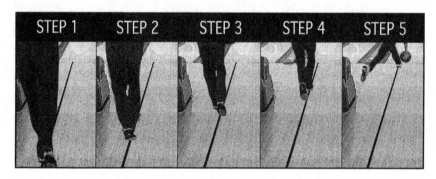

Fig. 3-9

Since I started working with Chris in 2009, he's continued to put up great numbers and extend his streak of consecutive BJI First-Team All-American appearances. In 2010-11 Chris started off the season by becoming just the sixth bowler in PBA history (joining Billy Hardwick, Johnny Petraglia, Pete Weber, Mike Aulby and Norm Duke) to win the Triple Crown when he took the PBA World Championship title over Bill O'Neill. Of course, I've never been one to take credit for the success of the bowlers I coach (they are the ones out there throwing the ball under all that pressure and with so much on the line after all), but to me, the ultimate satisfaction is seeing the people I help reach their goals and live their dreams out on the lanes.

4

Why Is My Timing Off and How Can I Fix It?

I have never helped make a bowler's release better by working directly on his release. Even though I've had literally hundreds of bowlers come to me complaining of a problem with their release, I have NEVER worked directly on the mechanics of a bowler's release to help him improve his game. On the other hand, I have helped fixed hundreds of releases by focusing on some other part of a bowler's game, such as his footwork, swing path, balance or timing. But when bowlers come to me, mired in a slump that they simply can't shake, they always insist that there is some problem with their release that is the cause of their suffering. "I'm thumbing it!" or "I'm dropping it!" or "I'm chicken-winging it!" or "I'm missing it!"[1] These are the universal phrases bowlers use to describe their afflictions (plus a few more that I can't print so as not to offend general audiences). When bowlers come to me with these worries, I

---

1 Or my personal favorite catch-all phrase: "I suck!"

listen, but I never look at the release itself[2] because I know that the true cause of the problem is somewhere else in the bowler's game – and it is always an issue related to balance or timing.

When I'm asked to describe why I don't spend a lot of time worrying about the release, my favorite response is to ask my inquisitor to think about the analogy of a jigsaw puzzle. I tell the person to go out and buy a thousand-piece jigsaw puzzle – it could be a meadow or a panoramic view of Lake Tahoe or a famous Van Gogh painting, it doesn't really matter much – lay down the pieces, and then try to put the center piece in first. When you get it, give me a call. If you've ever done a jigsaw puzzle, you know that this is impossible – and that the way any reasonable person assembles a jigsaw puzzle is to start with the border pieces and then work their way in. That's essentially the way I coach; I build a foundation with solid footwork, a straight swing, good timing and balance and then fill in the smaller pieces (like the release) at the end. Once you have the fundamentals in place, then working on your release[3]is more a matter of fine-tuning your game or learning new tricks than it is building it in the first place.

Although our last chapter on consistent direction was important, this chapter, which deals with rhythm, balance and timing, is what I feel is my most innovative departure from traditional coaching theories. From a coaching standpoint, it's not super-hard to get a bowler to improve from a 120 average to 160, but getting someone who's averaging 180 up to a 200 –

---

2   The only time I might look at the release is to help me to more quickly identify the cause of the problem, since certain release moves tend to point to certain categories of timing or balance issues.

3   I work on new releases with Tour players all the time. But these bowlers are already so fundamentally sound that this kind of work is usually to establish new "tricks" that can be used on certain conditions where that particular player is looking for a new way to attack.

or even a 220 average, or taking a good pro and making him a great one is much more difficult; and the things you almost always have to work on in order to achieve it are more consistent timing and balance. The reason this part of coaching is so difficult is that most good bowlers already have fairly consistent direction, so it is a lot harder to find obvious flaws in their games to hone in on, correct and improve.

This is where I feel like I've come up with a much simpler, much more logical way to diagnose the timing and balance flaws that keep bowlers from reaching their full potential. I start by assessing the bowler's rhythm by determining where the majority of his effort is spent. Does he use too much effort getting the ball into the swing? Is there a long pause between steps that kills the momentum of the ball? Is he using more upper body than lower body strength? Once I determine that, then I move on to the timing spot to see if the bowler matches. If he doesn't then I must determine the cause, which is always related to one of two components: the spine tilt or the pivot step. Finally, I'll have a look at the bowler's release point to be sure that the swing is "flat[4]," that the ball is coming off of the hand at a consistent spot, and that the point where the ball comes in contact with the lane is in the same place time after time. Once everything is clicking, you should feel like you are able to throw the ball with complete control – but it all starts by having a look and understanding your misses from the side.

The Speed Control Miss

The first way for a bowler to start the ball on the same target line as he did on a "perfect" shot and still miss at

---

4   Also known as the mythical term "the flat spot" which we'll discuss and describe in detail.

the pins is to throw the ball faster or slower[5]. There are any number of reasons that might cause a bowler to increase or decrease his speed from normal, but the most common way I see is when the bowler's weight distribution is out of position (we'll get into what those positions are exactly in a moment), forcing him to lunge up or down with the head, shoulders and torso. This causes the swing to either lose or gain tension and, consequently, momentum. Probably the best way to visualize this is to imagine a ball swinging on the end of a string. Think about what would happen if the end of the string opposite the ball were to suddenly move up, down, left or right. The tension on the string would change and the speed (and possibly, the direction) of the ball would either decrease or increase. The same thing happens when a bowler moves his body during the swing. Moving the shoulder (the end of the string) closer to the ball will cause it to hook earlier because it reduces the tension and decreases speed, while moving the shoulder further away causes it to hook later for the opposite reason.

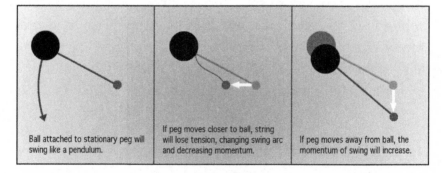

Ball attached to stationary peg will swing like a pendulum.

If peg moves closer to ball, string will lose tension, changing swing arc and decreasing momentum.

If peg moves away from ball, the momentum of swing will increase.

Fig. 4-1

---

5 The "faster" shot would miss light and the "slower" shot would miss high.

The Rev Rate Miss

Another way to miss on a shot that starts on-line is if your rev rate were to increase or decrease from normal. The way this typically happens is that the ball comes off your hand at a different release point. If the ball comes off later than it did on your strike shot, your rev rate will increase (due to your hand rotating for that extra fraction of a second prior to release). On the flipside, if the ball comes off your hand slightly sooner, your rev rate will decrease because your hand spent slightly less time rotating the ball. Usually, these problems are created earlier in the approach, but they are always due to some issue related to timing, and the only way to accurately diagnose this is by looking from the side.

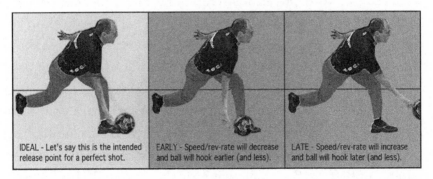

IDEAL - Let's say this is the intended release point for a perfect shot. | EARLY - Speed/rev-rate will decrease and ball will hook earlier (and less). | LATE - Speed/rev-rate will increase and ball will hook later (and less).

Fig. 4-2

Camera Position from the Side

Before we move on and look at the many reasons that cause these timing and balance-related misses, I'd also like to note that, from the side, I prefer to set up the camera one lane over (a lane to the right for right-handers and to the left for left-handers) facing the bowler's throwing side. I position the camera adjacent to the point where the timing spot occurs, so that when the bowler is in his stance the camera is turned toward him and then follows as he makes his way to the foul line. I also like to get the camera at head-level, because that helps me to see the weight transfer from top to bottom from a better perspective.

Cutting You in Half from Top to Bottom and Front to Back

Has the phrase, "I'm going to give it 110%" always bothered you as much as it has me? Good, because in bowling, when it comes to breaking down the amount of effort used in throwing a shot, all anyone's got is 100%. That's not to say that you need to use all of your physical strength and effort to throw a shot – some people only require 50 or 60 percent of their effort to throw the ball. What I'm saying instead is that, on a given shot, we can break down what percentage of our effort *on that particular shot* went where. Looking at you from top to bottom, how much of your effort on a given shot came from your legs versus your upper body? Then, watching you from the start of the approach to the finish, where did you expend the greatest amount of effort: the pushaway? The backswing? The release? The follow-through?

Since I spent a lot of time in the last chapter explaining that I believe footwork is the more "fundamental" fundamental than the swing, then you shouldn't be too surprised to find out that I like to see bowlers use a much higher percentage of their effort in their lower bodies than their upper bodies. I prefer to see the distribution of effort between the upper body and the lower body in the ballpark of 30 percent and 70 percent, respectively. What this means is that the kind of physical game I believe to be the most consistent (and again, this is based on facts and evidence supported by the kinds of fundamentals you see among the overwhelming majority of modern bowlers in the Hall of Fame) is one that relies more heavily on lower body strength to throw the ball. And the Hall of Fame isn't the only authority that seems to prefer fundamentals that favor a higher percentage of effort from your lower body – other sports seem to favor players who use their lower bodies more than their upper bodies as well.

Let's take boxing for instance. If you've ever studied that sport, you'll know that boxing trainers always teach their students to "load up" and to "throw a punch from the ground up." What they mean by this is that, in order to throw the hardest punch possible, it's best for a boxer to set himself with his weight on his back foot, then to start the punch from the back leg, transferring his weight and energy from the back leg, into the arm, then through the target. If you don't believe me, then try challenging another person to a contest where you take turns punching each other. First, you punch the other guy while falling back away from him with your feet coming up off the ground. Then, let him punch you after planting his legs and throwing the punch going forward. I guarantee you this will not be a fun experience for you. I'm joking, of course, but the same truth applies to bowling. Bowlers who use their lower bodies in greater proportion to their upper bodies tend to throw the ball more powerfully and more consistently than those who don't. In my experience, the pros bowl this way and the bowlers who struggle and are looking to come to me for help often tend to not.

The other test you can use to prove this theory is what I

call "The Skinny Forearms" principle. One physical similarity that you tend to find between nearly every great bowler[6] is that their forearms are skinny and there is not much difference between the size of the forearm on their throwing arm and their non-throwing arm. If you shake hands with Parker Bohn III or Dave Husted or Chris Barnes or Mika Koivuniemi, you'll be shocked to see that, in spite of bowling tens of thousands of games since childhood, that their arms are pretty much exactly the same size. Compare this to tennis players like Rafael Nadal or Rod Laver, who each have disproportionately larger forearms on the arm that holds their tennis racquet. Why do the greatest pro bowlers in the world have such skinny forearms then? Because they let their legs do the majority of the work! Remember: legs are for power. The arm is for direction.

100% from Front to Back

When it comes to breaking down the amount of effort from the start of the approach to the finish, my preference is that as much of a bowler's effort as possible is conserved for the pivot step, release and follow-through, which means that your stance and pushaway (and any number of steps during which they are executed) should expend as little effort as possible. Probably the two best players of all time at conserving as much of their effort as possible until the final step are Walter Ray Williams, Jr. and Pete Weber.

With Walter, his first two steps are about as close to someone casually walking down the street as possible. His stance is perfectly relaxed, with the ball cradled in towards

---

6   The main exceptions here are Wayne Webb, Brian Voss, Mike Durbin and Jim Godman - each of those guys had studly, arm-wrestler forearms!

the body to offset the weight. As the steps commence, all of Walter's energy is conserved until his final, explosive last step, where he throws the ball with just about everything he's got, right along his target path. As he comes through the ball, Walter has an extremely unusual move where his left arm extends completely behind his back while his right arm fires through, almost touching the left arm behind him at the peak of the follow through. Because he saves so much of his effort for the finish, Walter Ray rarely ever throws poor shots under pressure, and it is probably safe to say that his is the most consistent finish ever – given his records as the all-time career titles and earnings leader in pro bowling history.

Pete, even though his style is virtually the antithesis of Walter[7], the two have clearly been the best bowlers on Tour since the mid 1980's. Pete's stance is just as natural, relaxed and easy as Walter's, and his move into his first few steps is completely effortless. Pete expends a little more energy than Walter in getting the ball to the top of his backswing, but he still reserves the bulk of it for the final move, where he snaps his shoulders and hips back to square and delivers the ball with tremendous power for someone who stands 5' 7" and weighs 135 pounds.

Even though I don't necessarily have a completely scientific means for assigning these percentages, I do feel that through observation it's fairly easy to break down how much energy is expended at certain parts of the approach and assign ballpark numbers to them. My recommendation is that no more than 20% of your effort is used in the stance and pushaway, which means that you'd then have 80% of your effort left to throw with. That's one of the biggest reasons why Walter and Pete are

---

7   Pete likes to throw the ball slow and hook it a lot while Walter likes to throw it hard and play very straight.

such great clutch players, because there is never any decelera-
tion during the release on a shot in which they absolutely need
to strike – because they've saved all of that effort for the critical
task of throwing the ball. So they never cut it short[8] (the most
common miss under pressure) when they need it! The moral of
the story? Save that effort for the finish because, no matter how
big or strong you are, you only get 100% on each shot!

The Relationship Between Foot Speed and Swing Speed

We've talked about what happens if you have slow feet
and a quick swing (it's not good, if you remember) but the
bigger picture is that in order to promote good balance and
maximize your consistency, your foot speed and your swing
speed should closely match. What this means is that the speed
of your footwork and the speed of your swing shouldn't be too
far apart (or out of sequence) and your foot speed should be
slightly greater than your swing speed. If they do happen to
be too far out of sequence, it will cause an overabundance of
upper body manipulation, a loss of balance, a lack of consistency and, sometimes, a greater susceptibility to injuries. If you
have slow feet, then it stands to reason that you should also
have a swing that is slightly slower. If your swing is fast, then
your feet need to be just a little faster. Why? Because if your
swing is fast and your feet are slow then your feet will have a
hard time keeping up with the momentum of your swing.

Another way of looking at this is through a very well-
known technique taught throughout the coaching world,
which is called "walking by the ball." The way I like to think of

---

8   This is kind of a catch-all phrase but the best description is David Ozio's
"Failure to finish the shot" explanation we discussed back in Chapter 2.

this is to envision the idea that even when the ball is going into the backswing, the motion of the footwork should be driving the ball forward – like it would if the ball were sitting in a car while you're driving down the road. What happens when the car stops suddenly? The ball keeps going forward, and will need something to stop it (like a seatbelt) or it is likely to go crashing through the windshield[9]. The point is, if you don't keep walking, then the ball will lose momentum and then something – namely your muscles – will be forced to get it back moving again. This is not a very good thing when it comes to generating power or making good, consistent shots because gravity is a lot more effective at generating momentum than your muscles are.

A lot of what determines these strategies has to do with your category of timing. If you're a member of the Tommy Jones timing category and you push the ball away early, you better have fast feet in order to keep up with the ball to remain in time. If you're one of the folks who pushes it late like Chris Barnes, then you'll want your feet to be slower in order to give the swing time to catch up. Try playing around with these adjustments in practice and see what works for you, remembering that the most important thing is to be sure that, whatever adjustment you make, that you're "in time" at the timing spot, which we'll discuss next.

The Timing Spot

We've already spent quite a bit of time describing the timing spot and the fact that bowlers who get there are usually pretty good, but we've yet to discuss the exact reasons why it is that

---

9   Which is also why it's always a good idea to keep your equipment in the trunk on the way to your local bowling center! Trust me on this one!

The Myth of Slow Feet

During one of my weekend clinics at Fountain Bowl, I met a woman who came right up to me and asked, "So, are you the big-time coach everyone keeps telling me about?"

"I guess?" I said, feeling the familiar pressure that comes with high expectations.

"Well, my friends and I joined a league at the beginning of this season and we're starting to get pretty fed up. I'm averaging 102 but I haven't made any improvement since the start of the year and I actually think I might be getting worse, if that's even possible. If things don't start to change by the end of the season, then we're done."

The woman looked to be in her mid-50's. She was pretty slight – about 5'3" and 105 pounds – and that's if I'm being rude. She was very well-dressed and reminded me that she was the kind of person who was used to being successful in life at whatever it was that she put her mind to.

"Let me see you throw a few shots." I told her.

After watching just one shot, the word that immediately came to mind was "glacial." This poor lady looked like her feet were stuck in cement and it literally seemed like it was taking 10 seconds from the start of her approach to the time the ball left her hand. I watched her throw a few more shots and her ball was going everywhere – the right gutter, the left gutter and every place in between. It just struck me how slow she was walking and, consequently, how much upper body she was using to throw the ball. This wasn't a bowling style, it was a Pilates workout – except there was even less of a payoff at the end – not to mention infinitely more humiliation!

I asked her, "Why is it that you're walking so slow?"

She replied, "Well, that's what some of the better bowlers

in the league keep telling me to do. They say that if I want to hit the pocket, I need to slow my feet down."

"Let me ask you a question about these so-called better bowlers. What are they averaging?"

"About 160."

"Well, take it from me, if they're averaging 160, then they're not exactly knocking the pocket down too impressively themselves."

I continued, "Take a look at me for a second. I'm 6'4", 260 pounds. I weigh more than two and a half of you. When I throw the ball, there's quite a bit of mass and weight behind it, so it might make sense for me to slow my feet down so I'm not throwing the ball so hard that it never has a chance to hook."[10]

I continued, "Have you ever thought that maybe you should *speed your feet up* to generate more momentum?"

"Well, how fast should I go?"

"I'm not saying you should run, but walk at least as fast as you would if you saw a new handbag at Nordstrom marked down 50 percent and wanted to beat the rush of fellow shoppers. Not exactly running. Just walking fast."

She liked that idea and picked it up immediately. Her first five shots trying it that way hit the headpin and resulted in three nine counts and two strikes. Her face lit up and she started having fun from that point on. Now, when I go to my weekend clinics at Fountain and she's there, when she sees me she says with a smile, "There's the big guy who helped

---

10   I didn't tell her this, but when I bowled on Tour, I was always working on slowing my feet down for just this reason – except in 1985 when the lanes hooked so much we had to throw Blue Dots every week just to hit the right side of the headpin. Not coincidentally, I led the PBA in average that year and, at the time, I became the only right-hander not in the Hall of Fame to lead the tour in average. As always, leave it to me to be a fly in the ointment and mess up the curve! But I digress.

me learn how to hit the headpin!" She's still a loyal Fountain Bowl customer and now bowls two leagues a week (plus the clinics) – and all because someone took the time to help her improve. Oh and by the way, you still think slowing your feet down is a good idea for everyone? Try speeding them up now and then and you might actually be surprised at the results!

bowlers tend to improve as they get closer to matching it. First, we'll take a look at a bowler who matches at the timing spot and dissect the reasons, from a timing and balance standpoint, why the positions promote good, consistent bowling. Next, we'll look at a bowler who is late and diagnose the problems that this kind of timing causes. Finally, we'll do the same for a bowler who is early (the most common category of amateur bowlers that I coach). As we go through the examples, see if you can pinpoint some of the problems you notice in your own game, and then track them back to their cause at the timing spot. If you can, it'll be a great head start when it comes to improving your own game!

Perfect Timing

By now we all know what this looks like (image left) but here, we'll actually go into the reasons why the associated positions lead to balance, consistency and over

IN TIME

Fig. 4-3

all good bowling. First of all, unless your swing never reaches parallel, every bowler's swing is parallel to the floor at some point on the downswing. The question is, where is your slide leg at the moment this occurs? If it's flat on the floor, then you're in good shape to throw your best shot. Why? Because you're in perfect balance! Your head is directly above your core, your spine is tilted slightly forward, your back (pivot) leg is driving forward and turning under to clear out space for the swing, your hips and shoulders are staying down at a consistent level and your arm is being thrust forward with the full momentum that everything around it has generated. The only thing left to do is to decide which way you want to run the shot out[11]!

Late Timing

As you'll remember, the most noteworthy exception to our timing rule when it comes to being late is Jason Couch. Now, unless you're as strong and possess as much god-given athletic talent and hand-eye coordination as Jason has, here is what is most likely to happen when you have late timing at the timing spot:

LATE TIMING

Fig. 4-4

---

11 Bowlers are known for their "body English" after throwing a shot to help coax it into going where they want it to go. Running it out is a very fancy expression of this, and pros usually only do it when they know there is a very good chance that the shot will strike. However, I've been known to run out a few two-pins (on shots I thought were going to strike) in my day, so it doesn't always work to perfection!

First, your head and shoulders are likely to be too far back in relation to your pivot step (which means your weight is also too far back), and you will either remain in this position throughout the release, whereby you will then dump the ball straight into the floor with nothing on it, or you'll throw your spine, head and shoulders forward violently during the release, causing your swing to accelerate and/or your hand to come out of the ball too late (just how late depends on your strength – typically the stronger you are, the later you will hold on). There really is no limit to the number of inconsistencies this creates, but typically, what I hear and see from bowlers who suffer from this problem is that their balance, direction and release are all very inconsistent.

Early Timing

Jason's Hall of Fame counterpart at the opposite end of the timing spectrum is Marshall Holman, who parlayed his early timing into one of the great careers in bowling history through amazing touch and super-human leg strength. For mere mortals, however, early timing usually leads to a lack of power at best (when the bowler doesn't try

EARLY TIMING

Fig. 4-5

to fight this weak position using upper body strength), and, at worst, inconsistent direction, balance and power in the case of the bowler who does attempt to use his upper body to compensate. This is the case because when the ball is coming down from the swing prior to the foot getting flat, there's not much time for the hand to do much to the ball, so the result is usually either a lack of ball speed, a low and/or inconsistent rev rate and poor direction due to the shoulder being thrown forward to generate more power. There are quite a few possible fixes when it comes to this problem, ranging from shortening or softening the pushaway (to get the swing started earlier) to walking by the ball and then speeding up the footwork (to give the ball more time to swing before the bowler reaches the slide). Usually, when viewing a bowler's game from the side, it is fairly obvious to see the point where the timing can be altered in a way that makes it as simple for the bowler (given his size, strength, athletic ability and other traits) to incorporate – and then repeat – as possible. Now, let's have a look at the two elements I focus on most to help bowlers get their timing to the spot.

Spine Tilt

The first piece I look at to test the consistency of your timing is spine tilt. This idea extends throughout the approach, keeping in mind that once you reach the timing spot and then all the way through the release, the spine tilt should remain as stable as possible. Until that point however, you'll see quite a bit of variation in the amount of spine tilt, even among really good bowlers. A bowler like Mike Fagan has a lot more spine tilt at the top of his extremely high backswing than a player like Dave Ferraro, who has an extremely low backswing. What makes both of these players great (and so extremely consistent) however, is two things. First, their spine tilt isn't so extreme at any point during their approach that it requires a change in the rhythm of the footwork and second, it doesn't cause the weight to be distributed disproportionately (from front to back or top to bottom) to a degree that would cause a loss of balance. If it is, it might be something I might suggest tweaking, but as long as it remains consistent throughout the release I'm probably not going to touch it.

Fig. 4-6

Good bowlers tend to keep their spine angle within five degrees between the peaks of their backswing all the way to their follow-through, meaning that as they are releasing the ball, their spines (and really, their entire bodies) are remaining in a stable position as the ball swings through. As I mentioned above, there is a large amount of variation from bowler to bowler when it comes to assigning exactly what that a good spine angle should be but, over the years, I've found it to be in the range of 30 to 55 degrees[12].

The reason the spine tilt is instrumental in promoting a

---

12 Bowlers with lower backswings tend to have less tilt, while bowlers with higher backswings tilt more. The biggest exception to this are two-handers who often use as much as 70 degrees of spine tilt due to their non-throwing hand remaining on the ball.

consistent release is related to the tension created by the relationship between your shoulder and your ball as it swings.
If your spine tilt varies, then the tension between your shoulder and the ball will vary, making it more difficult to time the
moment when the ball ideally comes off of your hand. If your
spine tilts forward, then your swing is going to get steeper and
faster, which, unless you have the strength of 50 mules to help
you hold on to the ball, is going to cause you to dump your
shot onto the lane very early with quite a bit of extra speed. On
the other hand, if the spine tilts back at the release, you're going to lose speed and hit up on the ball, which has the dreaded
double effect of causing the ball to hook very early and burn up
too much of its energy before it hits the pins (a really bad thing
when the lanes are hooking a lot). So your best bet is to hold
that spine angle constant, which is something that should start
as early as the stance and the pushaway. You'll want to pre-set
your spine tilt at the start by leaning ever so slightly forward
during the stance (remembering what we said about keeping
your stance relaxed and easy), without allowing your weight
to go too far forward as you push the ball and commence your

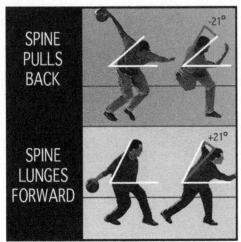

Fig. 4-7

swing. As the ball reaches
the peak of your swing,
your spine tilt is prob-
ably going to go forward
some amount, then back
some as the ball comes
through into the release.
But as long as you are
able to get your spine tilt
within the ranges I men-
tioned above from the
peak of your backswing
through the release (30-55

degrees with no more than five degrees of variation from start to finish), then you are going to be well on your way to becoming a very good, very consistent bowler.

Pivot Step

We've already seen why this step is important from a direction standpoint (to clear space for the ball to swing through and to help promote lateral balance), but it's also absolutely instrumental from a timing standpoint as well. The reason for this is that the position of the pivot step in relation to the head is the biggest determining factor in evaluating balance and, consequently, everything else that comes after it. The hallmark of a good pivot step is that it is as close to directly under the head as possible. The reason for this is because if the pivot step is too far forward (past the head), then the weight tends to be distributed too far back, causing a lunge down and forward with the upper body in order to generate power. In this case the lunge causes the spine (and the head, which is attached) to tilt forward, which then causes the swing to get steep (because it's attached at the shoulder, which also moves with the upper body) and the ball to come off of the hand early – usually with a very low rev rate and poor direction. On the other hand, if the step is too far back (behind the head), then the weight tends to get too far forward and the bowler lunges up and back with the upper body, causing the spine, head and shoulder to tilt back, which saps the momentum of the swing and can also lead to hitting up on the ball.[13]

The other key component to a good pivot step that

---

13   Hitting up on the ball is exactly what it sounds like. It happens when the fingers come out of the ball as the swing is on its way up. The ramifications are that the ball tends to hook earlier and either goes high or uses up too much of its energy before it hits the pins, leading to poor carry percentage.

promotes consistent speed control and rev rate is that the hips remain level all the way from the start of the slide until the follow through. You'll notice that when your hips stay down, with little or no movement from start to finish, it allows you to keep your center of gravity low all the way through the release, allowing you to generate a great deal of power and momentum into the ball. It also – since the hips are directly connected to the shoulders – allows you to keep the right shoulder down so that the ball can be delivered underneath the head, along the intended target path. This will also help keep the angle of your hips closely matching the angle of your shoulders at the point of release. The way you can check how this feels is to get into a good finish position without the bowling ball and see what happens with the mobility and flexibility of your shoulders when you transition from your pivot step into the slide. You'll notice that because your hips are attached to your shoulders, when they stay down, your shoulders have a hard time rotating – it will almost seem as if your shoulders are locked into place, making it almost physically impossible to over-rotate your shoulders.

The opposite of this is the bowler who lifts his hips up during the pivot step and through the release, causing the weight to shift from the lower body to the upper body. This almost always causes the shoulder and head to go forward, putting the bowler in a weak position to deliver the ball. All of these problems we've just illustrated will always manifest in a release that just doesn't feel right – and what we're about to discuss next is the last piece of the puzzle: the release point.

But before we look at that, one other item I look for when it comes to the pivot step is where on the approach it takes place. On most modern synthetic approaches there is a splice that occurs just past the end of the ball return that I like to use to determine whether or not the pivot step is too far back, too far forward or just right. The most common problem area I see among lower-average bowlers is that the pivot step takes place too far behind this splice, forcing them to lunge forward in a last-ditch attempt to get all the way to the foul line. This has the tendency to throw the weight up and forward, causing many of the timing and balance problems I mentioned above. Interestingly enough, Chris Barnes is one of the exceptions to this rule – as he initiates his slide about 18 inches behind the splice. The reason Chris gets away with this is because he has extremely long legs[14], and he also happens to be very strong and athletic. On the other end of the spectrum are the bowlers whose pivot step occurs past the splice, forcing them to decelerate and pull back at the finish to avoid going over the foul line. The trick is to get that pivot step as close to the splice as possible, so you can get to the foul line naturally, in a strong position that complements your rhythm and timing.

The Release Point

So we've seen the main issues that sometimes cause bowlers to be out of position at the timing spot and, ultimately, during the release, but what is it about maintaining your spine angle and your hip level during the pivot step that fixes your release and allows you to throw the ball like the pros? Why is it that the pros can not only hit within a board right or a board left of their target line shot after shot (you saw why in Chapter 3), but also keep their speed within a quarter mile per hour and their rev rate within 20 RPM? Well, it has to do with an almost mystical term that is sometimes overused and often misunder-

---

14   Chris has a 36" inseam, making it very hard for him to find Levi's that fit!

stood by bowlers and students of the game the world over: The Flat Spot.

The Flat Spot

Probably the simplest way I've come up with to describe the flat spot is that it is "the line made by the two points represented by the position of your hand at the bottom of the swing and at the release." Conceptually, a lot of people consider these points to be one and the same (and sometimes, they are), but if you factor in the concept that the bowler is moving forward as the release is unfolding, the swing is no longer a circular arc, but instead an oblong shape that is much flatter at the bottom. To explain this further, imagine that you are standing still at the foul line and swinging the ball from the stance, into the backswing, and then releasing it out onto the lane. If you were to track the path of the ball as it swings, the resulting shape it would form would look like a perfect, circular letter "C". Now, let's assume the bowler makes the same motion, except imagine that the bowler is no longer standing stationary, but moving forward. Now, the path that the ball makes looks more like a sideways "U" with the "flat spot" located along the bottom. Now, imagine the bowler's torso (and hence, the ball) moving all over the place during the swing. You could create all kinds of funny shapes, none of which will have that nice, even flat spot along the bottom that the best bowlers tend to create.

What the flat spot allows is for some margin of error to be built into the release. Using our prior visual examples, let's imagine what happens if our bowler with the circular swing releases the ball at three different points. On the first shot, the ball comes off the hand precisely at the bottom and lands at a given point on the lane. On the second shot, the ball comes off of his hand sooner, and lands on the lane at a point much closer to the bowler. On the third shot, the ball comes off his hand after the bottom of the arc, (i.e. on its way back up) which makes the ball travel much further out onto the lane than his first shot. If the bowler has a long flat spot, however, these three varying points of release will actually hit the lane much closer to one another than they did in our circular swing example. The result? Improved consistency. And it all comes from holding the position of your spine and the level of your hips from the peak of your backswing through the release.

Where the Ball Comes off Your Hand

The next thing I look at when it comes to the release point is where the ball is coming off of your hand in relation to the swing. We talked earlier about how some coaches even prefer to measure timing based on this point, and how that system never really worked for me because there was so much variation among the spots from which large samples of really good bowlers release it. But the one thing that all of these good bowlers do is that, much as we saw with the spine tilt, there is a window in which these bowlers release it from, and, individually, they all happen to be extremely consistent with releasing the ball from the same spot time after time.

So why is it important that the ball comes off the hand at the same spot every time? Well, for a number of reasons actually. First, the earlier the ball comes off your hand, the earlier it will start to hook, so if you put the ball on the lane at five feet over the foul line on one shot, then drop it three feet onto the lane the next, the ball is in contact with the lane for two extra feet on the second shot, which will cause it to hook early. From another standpoint, the longer the ball stays on your hand, the more rotation you will create, so, assuming your ball speed is the same, the shot with more rotation will hook earlier than

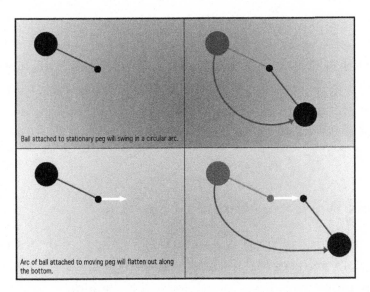

Ball attached to stationary peg will swing in a circular arc.

Arc of ball attached to moving peg will flatten out along the bottom.

Fig. 4-8

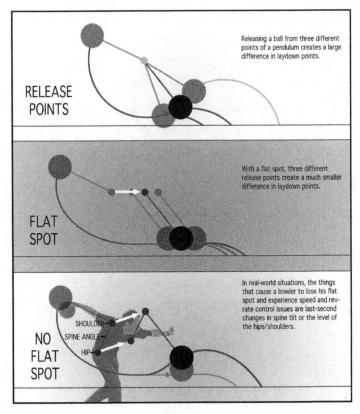

RELEASE POINTS

Releasing a ball from three different points of a pendulum creates a large difference in laydown points.

FLAT SPOT

With a flat spot, three different release points create a much smaller difference in laydown points.

NO FLAT SPOT

SHOULDER
SPINE ANGLE
HIP

In real-world situations, the things that cause a bowler to lose his flat spot and experience speed and rev-rate control issues are last-second changes in spine tilt or the level of the hips/shoulders.

Fig. 4-9

the shot that came off of your hand sooner. Usually, these problems are caused by something that is happening sooner in the delivery (such as a short pivot step or footwork that doesn't match the speed of the swing) but, whatever the case, the more consistently you can get the ball off of your hand in the right spot during the release, the more consistent you will be as a bowler.

Pros Work the Middle of the Ball

If you watch slow-motion video of a bunch of professional bowlers' releases from behind, the thing you'll notice most is how all of them keep their hands in the middle of the ball[15]. More specifically, their hands tend to stay in the center of the ball vertically, while remaining close to the equator in the horizontal direction. During the final moments before the release, they rotate their wrist around a small swath of the ball as their arm comes through, all the while keeping the forearm pointed ahead and moving straight along the intended target line. Most people consider this a release move but, as we've mentioned before, this is more a function of being in good position with respect to footwork, swing path, direction and balance.

Another thing the pros do during this release move is that they do not rotate their forearms with their wrists and hands. Instead, the inside part of the forearm (the side that faces in toward your body when you hold your arms relaxed at your side) faces the target all the way from the start of the release, continuing to the follow-through. This is what gives the pros

---

15   A term I hear a lot is "working the inside of the ball," which suggests that better bowlers keep their hands to the left side of the ball through the release. If you watch video of the top players, however, it is true that a lot of them start the downswing with their hands in that position, but by the time they release it, their hands are usually closer to the center.

such great direction, power and consistency because, even though they are putting a great deal of rotation on the ball, their arms are projecting the ball straight along the intended target path, which is then usually followed by the signature "arm-swinging-back-and-forth" move that all good bowlers do after they've thrown their best shot.

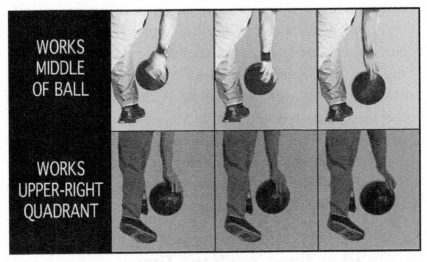

Fig. 4-10

Where the Ball Hits the Lane

If you were to ask Chris Barnes to throw 100 shots alongside a typical 160-average bowler and then look at an overhead graph that plotted all of the points where each and every one of their shots hit the lane, you'd end up with two distinct circles. Chris Barnes' circle would be about the size of a half-dollar. The 160-bowler's circle would be about the size of a dinner plate. That's because Chris Barnes' release point (not to mention his direction) is going to be much more consistent than his 160-average counterpart (and you would hope so considering Chris bowls for his living). This isn't much different than the wear pattern you might see on the faces of two 6-irons owned by a pro and a 20-handicap golfer. Over time, the pro will wear out a spot about the size of a dime, right in the center of the clubface (the sweet spot) while the 20-handicapper will beat up the entire surface area of the clubface and probably never even create a single, consistent wear spot.

The advantages this creates for Chris over time are obvious, but it is worth mentioning the subject because this test is something I will actually use to diagnose an issue with the release point (when that issue is not direction or timing-related, of course). If I do happen to notice a bowler's ball hitting the lane at varying points over a series of shots I'll know that there is a problem with the release point, and then begin looking at other things (such as spine tilt, hip level or footwork) to determine where the inconsistency is occurring. Once this spot is identified and the bowler takes steps to correct it, the point where the ball hits the lane always becomes more consistent.

If You're in Time, You Have Time

Since I've started coaching Bill O'Neill, we've developed a pretty familiar pattern of working together. The pattern is this: I pretty much leave Bill alone and when he needs some help (which is happening less and less frequently as time goes by) he comes to me. It's always the same thing these days[16], which Bill sums up as, "When I get it right it hangs, when I get it left it hooks. I don't have any time at the bottom." The cause of this problem varies (sometimes it's the length of his pushaway, other times it is caused by pulling the ball back into the swing and, occasionally, his third step will get a little slow), but you

---

16   Although early in our relationship it was something else – more on that in the case study for our next chapter.

can see it very clearly when you look at Bill's swing from the timing spot to the release point. What happens is that his swing gets a little late, causing it to come down at a steeper angle at the bottom, which eliminates his flat spot and doesn't give him any time at the bottom of the swing to rotate his hand like he normally does. When the ball comes off his hand a little early, he loses some of his rotation, causing the ball to miss light. When he releases the ball a little later, the extra rotation that generates causes the ball to hook high.

When Bill is on, his swing is completely flat at the bottom, which allows him to get away with these slight misses and to feel as if he can miss a little bit to the right and still get the ball back, and also miss a little bit left and get the ball to hold it's line. When you give someone the caliber of Bill O'Neill the ability to miss a board left and a board right of his target and still strike, there are going to be some serious scores shot on the lanes that day. And when Bill and I work together, after we identify the issue causing his lack of time at the bottom (which usually takes all of five to twenty minutes because he's so good at incorporating my suggestions and executing them on the fly), once he sees one miss right and hook back to the pocket and then one miss left and hold pocket he'll say, "I'm good Bakes. I've got all the time in the world now." So when you're in time, you have time. Unless you happen to be Bill's opponent, then time is definitely not on your side when he's on top of his game.

Chapter Summary

Hopefully, after reading this chapter, you've come over to my side in the whole "the-release-is-everything-versus-the-release-is-nothing" debate. The release is considered such an important piece of the puzzle by most bowlers because that is the last thing they feel when they throw the ball. But in reality, the release is merely a by-product of the kind of fundamentals a bowler exhibits throughout the course of his entire delivery – essentially, it is the last piece in the jigsaw puzzle – something you'd never dream of trying to put in place first. Before we move on to our final chapter, let's review what we've learned here:

- The release is the last piece of the puzzle when it comes to good fundamentals. Usually, when you do every-thing else right, the release just happens naturally!

- We look at the bowler from the side to diagnose issues that cause inconsistent speed control and rev rate.

- I primarily focus on two main elements when it comes to helping a bowler improve his timing: Spine Tilt and the Pivot Step.

- If your spine tilt is somewhere between 30 and 55 degrees and does not vary more than five degrees from the peak of your backswing to the release, your consis-tency will improve dramatically.

- If your pivot step is under your head and your hips remain level into the slide and the release, your consis-tency will also improve.

- Having a longer flat spot gives you a lot more margin for error in your release than you'll have if your swing is steep or shallow.

- Pros work the middle of the ball, while amateurs tend to release the ball from the upper-right quadrant.

- If you're in time, you have time.

Case Study #4
Fixing Mika's Pivot Step

Chris Barnes' roommate and one of his best friends out on the PBA Tour is Mika Koivuniemi, a player who most bowling experts feel is the best bowler ever to come out of Europe[17]. Mika was an international superstar before he came out on Tour in 1999, and won his first title in the ABC Masters (now the USBC Masters) in 2000. He won the U.S. Open in 2001, which earned him the nickname "Major Mika" and he then put together one of the best seasons in PBA history in 2002-2003, when he earned PBA Player of the Year and rolled a 300 game on national television. He continued as one of the Tour's dominant players through 2008, but had a rough season (by his standards)[18] in 2008-2009 and again in 2009-2010, only making two TV appearances over that stretch.

Before the 2010 PBA Tournament of Champions, Barnes visited me at Fountain Bowl with Mika tagging along. Mika asked if I could have a look at his game, so I spent some time filming him to see what his timing looked like[19]. What I showed

---

17   Mika originally hails from Finland, but now lives in Michigan.

18   Mika was 15th in earnings in 2008-2009 and 20th in 2009-2010. Not bad at all, but not nearly what Mika expected from himself.

19   While we were practicing, there were birthday parties on both sides of us. After a few games, one of the moms asks me, "The really serious guy just had a 300 and the other one has like 27 strikes in a row. Who are these guys?" My answer: "One is the best bowler in the world and the other is the best bowler in the history of Europe." Her reply: "What are they doing here?!"

him was that his timing was early and his pivot step had gotten just a little short (not quite under his head) which was causing him to come up just a bit at the line. This was then causing him to release the ball a fraction late, which made his ball burn up too much energy in the front part of the lane, which gave him a hard time getting the ball back from further to the right, as well as leaving more 10-pins than he was used to leaving. I told him that I thought if he could get his pivot step a little bit more under his head, that his hips would stay down, his release point would come a little sooner and his ball would store a little bit more energy to give him that extra back-end hook and accompanying improved pin carry he was looking for[20].

I didn't work with Mika again the entire off-season, but when he came back for the 2010-2011 PBA Tour season it was clear that he was a totally different bowler. Mika had his best season ever, becoming the first player in PBA history to qualify for the TV finals of each of the four PBA majors in a single season. In one of those shows, he put on one of the most iconic performances ever, rolling a 299[21] and a 267 game to win the biggest prize in bowling history[22]. Mika ended up winning his second PBA Player of the Year award by a landslide and his season-ending earnings ranked 3rd all-time.

When I had a chance to film Mika again, it was clear that he had worked on exactly what we'd talked about back at the 2010 Tournament of Champions. His pivot step was now directly under his head, his hips were staying level through the release

---

20   Chris and Mika both had pretty good weeks after that practice session – Chris led and Mika finished 3rd and they both lost to Kelly Kulick in one of the most memorable performances in bowling history.

21   He left a 10-pin on the final ball. He also set a record for the biggest margin of victory ever, winning 299-100 over Tom Daugherty.

22   $250,000. First prize for winning the PBA Tournament of Champions that season.

and the ball was coming off his hand just a bit sooner. Consequently, Mika was able to generate more area on the lane than anyone else, his pin carry had improved and he was still as deadly accurate as he had always been. It's no wonder Chris Barnes said he was the best bowler in the world prior to that year's World Series of Bowling even after everyone else had begun to write him off. And Mika definitely lived up to his "Major" nickname that year!

Fig 4-11

5

How Can I Tell When Everything's Going Right?

Over the last four chapters, we've seen in detail how direction, balance, timing and generating momentum are absolutely fundamental when it comes to improving your ability to play the sport of bowling[1]. When you do everything in a way that is fundamentally sound according to what we've discussed so far, you'll suddenly begin to notice a set of things you now have in common with other good bowlers. But most bowlers aren't going to have the luxury of carrying a video camera around with them every time they bowl (let alone an expert bowling coach) to help analyze every single thing they are doing wrong (or right). So how (besides your score), are you supposed to know for sure when things are going your way out on the lanes? That's where the similarities we're about to discuss come into play – and they always show up in a number of different places. Learning to read the symptoms of these similarities will indicate whether or not your bowling

---

1   In my book, that is irrefutable proof that bowling is a sport!

excursion will be smooth sailing or a tough grind, and will eventually allow you to build an awareness of how well you're bowling at a given moment. This awareness will then help you get through those tough times quickly before they can develop into a full-blown slump.

Since the sport of bowling is made up of three main categories of variables (the physical game, lane play and equipment) learning to control your physical game by throwing the most consistent shots possible will help you eliminate one of those variables (you!) so you can simply focus on lane play and equipment adjustments. If you've been bowling for any significant period of time at all, you understand that the lanes don't always play the same – even the same pair of lanes at your home bowling center could play radically different from one day to the next, or even one game to the next – so knowing that you're throwing the ball consistently will immediately inform you that when the same line you played yesterday with the same ball is now missing the pocket by five boards right, all you need to do is either make a move on the lane or switch to a ball that hooks more.

Finally, we all want to be one of the "cool kids" and, in the sport of bowling, the cool kids are the pros. We all want to throw it like them, and the purpose of this book up to this point has been to help you to identify the key fundamentals shared by the pros that you can incorporate into your game to produce better results than you've ever experienced. But what are the things that the pros have in common once the ball has left their hands that can help them determine whether or not their physical game is clicking on all cylinders at a given time? Let's have a look at those now.

Balance: The Universal Finish Position

When a good bowler throws a great shot, even though there are literally as many styles out there as there are bowlers, they pretty much all look exactly the same when they're finished. What this looks like is this: their weight is balanced perfectly on top of the left leg, the head and shoulders are behind the knee, the throwing arm is swinging freely back and forth with the front of the forearm facing directly at the target, and the pivot leg is extended out to the left with the foot turned down towards the floor. That's exactly what I used to see week in and week out when I was on Tour bowling against Marshall Holman, Earl Anthony, Mark Roth, Mike Aulby, Pete Weber, Dave Husted, David Ozio, Parker Bohn III and Del Ballard, Jr. That is what Barry Asher saw when he was out on Tour a generation before me and that is what Chris Barnes, Tommy Jones, Mika Koivuniemi, Jason Couch and Bill O'Neill see out on Tour now.

For bowlers who haven't quite yet reached that level, the finish position can encompass all sorts of interesting, telltale configurations – from the lean-back, to the lean-forward, to the fall-off, to the fake-post. All of these positions are signs that something is not right somewhere in the physical game, all of them have their own unique origins, and all of them require some form of tension or muscle manipulation in order to repeat, which makes them all inherently less consistent than the perfectly balanced, mechanically efficient finishes exhibited by the pros.

So if the finishing position is such a telling sign of the physical game's soundness, why don't I use it as the point from which I measure a bowler's timing? Well, that's because the pros are simply too good at faking it. As we've discussed before, bowlers typically report the most feedback from a shot during the release point. Really good bowlers know exactly what a great shot feels like and what their bodies do during the finish position after the ball has left their hands. So, most of the time, when a good bowler is off it is often by such a small margin that it is not enough to throw them off balance at the finish. But on the demanding conditions of tournament bowling, these small mistakes are often the difference between strikes and 2-8-10s and big fours, which, at the wrong time, can cost you making the cut, making it to TV or winning the title. And if you were to just look at the bowler's finish position on those few shots that went awry, there is usually no way to tell the difference between them and the perfect shot because the bowler is usually able to "fake" the finish position in his last-ditch attempt to "save" a shot that is headed off line.

When it comes to bowlers that haven't yet reached the pro level, the finish position tells me that there is an issue with balance – and the telltale sign of that is what I call "falling off" the shot. Falling off the shot is the most common sign of poor balance, typically caused by the bowler's weight transferring from the core (lower body) into the shoulders (upper body). This is always a symptom of early timing and a pivot step that is does not come under the head (from the side). When this happens, the bowler tries to generate power with his shoulder, so the right hip goes up, shifting the weight to the left leg, then the shoulder comes forward and the weight comes with it, causing a weak position at the release point and ultimately causing the bowler to step off to the right to avoid his weight carrying him past the foul line. This is also one of the biggest reasons why amateurs struggle to generate the kind of power the pros generate so effortlessly.

Head is well in front of pivot step.   Timing is early and spine tilt has shifted back.   Bowler loses balance and falls off to the right.

Fig 5-1

When it all happens perfectly, however, I call it "The Matrix Move." "The Matrix Move" is a term I coined to describe the finish of a perfect shot[2] from behind. After watching as much bowling as I have over the years, when a good bowler throws the ball just right it's almost as if I'm able to see the sequence of events from behind in slow motion. The move starts as the player is going into the slide step as the ball starts it's descent from the top of the backswing. As the ball comes down the swing path into the flat spot, the right foot makes a very quick flipping motion and veers left to clear an easy path for the ball. Right as this happens, the weight begins to shift from the right foot to the left and the ball goes hurtling by the ankle. As the follow through whips by the right ear, the right leg stays low (but not on the ground) and the player remains in perfect balance as the ball tracks right along the intended target path. The other thing that happens is that the spine angle remains constant from the start of the pivot step all the way until the follow through and, in the best cases, until the ball is two-

_____

2   Named for the movie "The Matrix", which, to the horror of my editor, I've never actually seen but know enough from the previews to feel comfortable using the name to describe this move.

thirds of the way down the lane[3]. As each of these steps in the sequence unfold, sometimes I even hear little sound effects!

| Slide is starting and ball is in perfect position. | Right foot spins under as hips and shoulders remain perfectly level. | Ball zips through as inside of arm chases ball through the target. Balance is perfect. |

Fig 5-2

From the side, there are a couple of big keys that illustrate the universal finish position, namely: the position of the head and shoulders in relation to the slide knee, the level of the hips, the amount of shoulder rotation, and the spine tilt. All of these elements are related, and if you see one going wrong it usually sets off a chain reaction causing each of the other pieces to falter as well. First of all, a good finish is marked by the head and shoulders positioned directly over the slide knee. If the head and shoulders are forward (or back, which is pretty rare), this is a sign that the bowler is out of time, causing him to lunge forward with the upper body in an attempt to generate power. As I've mentioned before, this position is almost always followed by a loss of balance and a step out to the right. Related to this is the position of the hips, which should remain level from the start of the slide through the release and follow-

---

3   This is what is referred to as "posting" a shot.

through. If the hips rise up at any point, then the shoulders and head will go with them, again affecting balance.

Lunging forward with the shoulders and head also contributes to another problem, which is over-rotating the shoulders. What you'll notice among the pros at the finish position is that their shoulders will remain square all the way from the release through the finish. When you lunge forward with your head and shoulders at the finish, inevitably you'll find yourself over-rotating your shoulders, which almost always results in a "pull" that goes left of target. As I outlined in Chapter 2, this is the most common miss in the sport of bowling and, if you can eliminate this miss through solid fundamentals, then you're sure to improve your scores. In addition to that, if you ever see this miss creeping up in your game, you'll have a great head start when it comes to understanding the reason for it and the first place to look to fix it – just look at your timing (it's going to be early) and the position of your pivot step (it's going to be short) in relation to your head!

Accuracy

One theory I have about what it takes to make it on the PBA Tour goes like this: you either have to be a stone-cold-shot-maker or you have to do something completely unique that no one else can do[4]. If you rank the all-time career PBA title winners by number of titles, then classify each of them as either "Stone-Cold-Shot-Maker" or "Unique," what you'll find

---

4   A stone-cold-shot-maker is someone who says, "Put the oil in the sprinkler system for all I care. Let's bowl!" Think: Walter Ray Williams, Jr. or Chris Barnes. A unique player is someone who says things like, "Oh, so they're going to let me throw it hard and hook it this week – see you at the pay window!" Think: Robert Smith. A few players in PBA history were actually both. They have a LOT of titles. Think: Mark Roth, Earl Anthony and Pete Weber.

is that the best of the best were members of the first category. Guys like Earl Anthony, Walter Ray Williams, Jr. Mark Roth, Pete Weber, Norm Duke, Don Johnson, Brian Voss – all players with 20-plus titles each – these were the greatest shot-makers of their era. And why were they the best shot-makers? Because they had the best fundamentals! Let's take Norm Duke, for example, who's probably considered by his peers on Tour today as the most accurate player.

Norm Duke is one of the best examples of excellent footwork in the history of bowling. He employs perfect crossover steps just prior to his pushaway and on the pivot step (both of which clear space for the ball to pass right under his head unimpeded), his steps are a fairly even length from start to finish, his pacing is consistent and his balance is as close to perfect as you will ever see[5]. Norm posts almost every shot, very rarely falling off balance, and is one of the most disciplined shot-makers in the history of the sport. Norm is always a threat at the U.S. Open (the tournament that demands the highest degree of accuracy) because it is contested on a dead flat[6] oil pattern every year and demands a complete command of a bowler's direction, speed and rev rate. He won the event for the second time in his career in 2011 and has several other high finishes in the prestigious tournament as well. But the thing that is the most interesting about Norm's finish position is that – even though he's just 5' 5" and weighs 135 pounds – you'd have a hard time knocking

---

5   When was the last time you saw Norm lose his balance or fall out of shot? You probably haven't – unless he happened to stick on the approach shooting a spare – and you may be waiting a long time before you'll ever see it happen again.

6   An oil pattern where the volume of oil is distributed evenly across the lane (a 1:1 ratio). All other PBA Tour patterns are between a 2:1 and 3:1 ratio, while a typical league pattern is approximately a 10:1 ratio. Most U.S. Open oil patterns are in the 40-foot range in terms of the length of the oil down the lane.

him over at the line because his finish position is so perfectly balanced.

Bowlers who have a hard time keeping their balance at the line, on the other hand, have a much more difficult time maintaining their accuracy (or, to use our term, direction). Sometimes they can get away with this if the lanes happen to be very forgiving, but on the more demanding sport patterns you see in tournaments[7], these flaws are sure to reveal themselves, always resulting in lower scores. It is also much more difficult for your eyes to track the path of your bowling ball[8] if your balance is poor, since your head is moving all over the place at the finish. On a more demanding condition, it is absolutely critical that you see the path of your ball in order to read exactly where a particular shot went in relation to what you were trying to do. Did you miss right because you drifted too far left? Or did your swing path come too far to the inside? If you fall off your shot and lose track of the board you slid on, how are you supposed to tell? The answer? If you can keep your balance at the line with good physical game fundamentals, then you're sure to notice a big improvement in your accuracy.

Turn Your Spin into Roll

In the last chapter, we talked about how pros tend to "work the middle of the ball" while amateurs work the "upper-right quadrant." In pro lingo, working the upper-right quadrant is called "spinning the ball," and when you hear a pro mention that he (or one of his fellow pros) is "spinning it," it's almost never in a good way. Although spinning the ball is sometimes

---

7 A typical league pattern has a 10:1 ratio of oil volume from the center part of the lane to the outside. Sport patterns are typically 3:1, or less.

8 Pros call this "picking the ball up."

helpful on extremely dry lane conditions, it is generally a product of a weak release resulting from poor direction, timing or balance. This really causes problems when the lanes are slick and/or require you to play a much straighter line to the pocket. In such situations, bowlers who are able to "roll" the ball more end-over-end are more likely to have success – mostly because this mode of attack allows them to play the straighter line to the pocket, as well as generate more hitting power at the pins. This will also help the ball hook earlier and more (and really, who doesn't like to see the ball hook more?) than it will throwing a spinner, and will also smooth out the shape of the ball's hook, allowing you to control the ball a lot more.

So how do you tell whether or not you're spinning the ball or rolling it? The best way to check is to look at your ball track after throwing a shot. Every time you throw the ball, when it comes back you'll notice rings of oil (or burn marks, depending on how much oil is on the lanes at a given time) on the left side of your finger and thumbholes. The further these rings are from the holes, the more likely it is that you're spinning the ball and, conversely, the closer they are to the holes, the more you're rolling it[9]. Most good bowlers track just left of the finger and thumbhole, while most amateurs tend to track much further away. Improving your direction, balance and timing will get your hand in a better position at the release point (more in the middle of the ball instead of in the upper right quadrant) and allow you to go from spinning the ball to rolling it like the pros.

---

9   The oil rings for people who spin the ball also tend to have a relatively small circumference. A player like Mike Fagan has a low track but a large track circumference, which means that he is "tilting it," rather than spinning it.

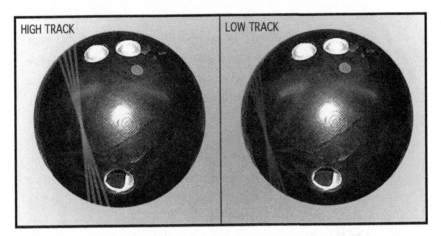

Fig. 5-3

Pete Weber – The Only Pre- and Post-Reactive-Resin Hall-Of-Famer

The advent of reactive-resin bowling balls in the early 1990's was one of the most revolutionary changes in the history of the sport of bowling. These bowling balls were probably the biggest factor in determining the way in which the sport is best played today, and for players to survive the change and continue their bowling careers, it required a number of significant adjustments. For some players, the advent of bowling balls that hooked so much more than anything that had yet been seen, was a welcome change. Walter Ray Williams, Jr. for example, was already an excellent player (he was the Player of the Year in 1986, well before reactive-resin) and considered virtually unbeatable on conditions where the shot was somewhere between the 1st and 7th boards prior to the advent of the new technology. But his career jumped through the stratosphere starting in 1993 (the year after the balls gained universal acceptance on Tour), a year in which he more than doubled his career titles (he started the year with six and ended it with 13 after winning seven titles on the season). He would then go on to win another 34 over the next 16 seasons and now is professional bowling's most prolific champion. The difference? Well, the balls allowed Walter Ray to compete from the 8th to 20th boards as well, making him a threat not only when the preferred shot was toward the outside, but also when the shot was in. That must not have been a very fun time out on Tour for the guys who used to dominate from the inside line.

On the other hand, Pete Weber, who had utterly dominated the Tour through the 1980's and early 1990's, compiling Hall of Fame statistics (19 career titles through the 1992 season) during that period, soon found himself at a big disadvantage with the advent of reactive resin. Pete dominated in the '80's because he had a unique trick that few other players could replicate, which was the ability to throw the ball with a tremendous amount of side rotation. What this did for Pete in the days of less aggressive bowling balls was that it allowed him to create a lot more mistake area on the lane as well as additional hitting power because his rotation was conducive to hooking much later and much harder on the back part of the lane than any other player. But reactive resin bowling balls hooked so much, that what was a unique, advantageous trait was now a disadvantage because Pete's ball now actually hooked too much on the back end, causing his misses to leave gaping splits that were nearly impossible to convert.

After experiencing two utterly dismal seasons in 1995 and 1996, Weber retooled his game and began figuring out how to compete with the new, more aggressive bowling balls. Exactly what Pete did was that he changed his swing, release and hip rotation in a way that allowed him to improve his direction and speed control while altering his rev rate and tilt in a way that allowed the bowling ball to "do the work." Specifically, Weber slowed down his hand and wrist rotation through the release, which cut down on the sharpness with which the ball changed direction[10]. He also slowed his hip and shoulder rotation (which had previously helped promote that fast release) to achieve the same ends. What this did in essence was that it turned Pete into a stone-cold-shot-maker!

The results? How about 16 more titles (bringing his career total to 35 – third on the all-time career list behind Williams and Earl Anthony) through the 2010-2011 PBA Tour season? Both halves of Pete's career are sufficient to earn him a spot in the Hall of Fame (Pete actually was already inducted in 1998) according to the criteria set by the PBA (a minimum of 10 PBA Tour titles or five titles with two majors). Would Walter Ray Williams Jr. have reached this level had reactive resin never been invented? Absolutely. But Weber is the only player who actually put up the numbers (and we're not even mentioning some of the greats whose careers fell by the wayside and never recovered after the appearance of reactive-resin – and believe me, there were quite a few). And all it took was a small change in fundamentals for Pete to do it.

---

10 In the pre-resin days, Weber's biggest advantage was his ability to get the ball to change direction and hook more on the back end than any other player on Tour. With reactive-resin, this became a huge disadvantage because it reduced his consistency both in hitting the pocket and carrying a high percentage of strikes on pocket hits.

Speed Kills (the Pins!)

One of the pros' best friends is the messenger shot, where a pin shoots from one sidewall to the other, taking out another pin that had stubbornly chosen not to fall after the ball's initial impact. Contrary to the generally held belief that a high rev rate yields messengers, the thing that really allows the pros to carry this hit is ball speed.[11] I've seen Walter Ray Williams, Jr. win plenty of titles with his 250-RPM rev-rate because he was throwing the ball hard enough to get a messenger to come through on a key shot.

The tricky thing about ball speed though, is that it usually requires increased foot speed, which sometimes makes it more difficult to keep one's balance at the finish. We already know that using your upper body to generate extra speed leads to direction and balance issues. We also know that sometimes bowlers actually tend to move their feet too slow in relation to their swing speed. So how fast is too fast when it comes to your footwork? I would suggest as fast as you can go without losing your balance as a good start. Anything that causes you to lose your balance is sure to be counterproductive because it hurts your accuracy as well as your ability to control your speed and rev rate consistently. You also want to be sure that your speed "matches" your rev rate. What I mean by this is that if you have (or want to have) a really high rev rate, you're going to need to have an equal amount of ball speed, otherwise your ball will hook so much that you'll never be able to control it. On the other hand, if your rev rate is low, you don't want to be throwing the ball "Mach 5," because then it will never hook.

---

11 Have you ever seen a little kid who can barely get the ball down the lane throw a messenger? I rest my case!

But whatever speed you can comfortably throw while remaining in balance is sure to help you kick a few more corner pins out with the messenger.

Get a Rev

Yes, I get it. You want to know how you can increase your rev rate! Well, the dirty little secret of this book is that if you improve your fundamentals, your rev rate will increase with it. Want to know why emerging PBA star Dan MacLelland has a 500-plus rev rate? It's because he combines a super-high backswing with superb fundamentals! Dan walks by the ball in his third step and swings it up over his head using very little effort. His upper body is very quiet as his hips drop down to start the downswing. The stability of the hips and lower body act as resistance as the ball starts to come through, the shoulders rotate naturally (this is key because you don't want to "throw" them forward because that will kill the momentum of the swing) and the arm and hand stay behind the ball, with the hand rotating through the equator. The lower body continues to remain stable as the ball is released, allowing the hand to fully rotate until the fingers, then the thumb, release from the ball. If you ever see Dan fall off a shot to the right, it might be the first. The combination of where the ball starts from the top of his swing and the way he releases it without impeding its momentum is a textbook example of how to maximize your rev rate.

Of course, we all don't possess the strength, flexibility and athleticism of Dan MacLelland, but we can all work on our fundamentals in order to maximize the rev rate that our own styles are capable of generating. A lower rev rate is often a sign of poor fundamentals, especially when it is combined with poor balance at the finish position. It never fails that when I am able to help someone to improve their fundamentals and their balance, the first thing they notice is that their rev rate has gone up too! Especially the guys!

The Pins Tell a Story Too

Yet another way to tell if you're on track is by watching how the pins fall. Any time you strike it's a good thing, but *how* you strike is sometimes just as important as whether or not the pins actually fell. As your game improves (especially your direction), inevitably you will begin to start feeling more and more "unlucky" because your misses are now likely to be "taps"[12] such as the 10-pin, 4-pin or 7-pin. But luck has very little to do with how the pins fall[13] or why it is you seem to be leaving more corner pins than usual. Pin carry has a lot more to do with the speed and angle that the ball is hitting the pins, which comes back to direction, speed control and rev-rate when you're talking about the things that you actually have control over as a bowler.

The most important hit I like to see as a coach is when the 10-pin is the last to fall – specifically when it is "snapped" off the deck by the 6-pin after that pin bounces off the right sidewall. On this hit, the ball enters the pins "3/4 pocket"[14] and usually has no issue carrying the other nine pins. The 10-pin, however, must be taken out by the 6-pin, whose only chance is to ricochet off the right sidewall at the correct angle to clip the 10-pin on it's way back off the deck. If the 6-pin is cut too

---

12   A "tap" is a shot that hits the pocket but still leaves one (or more) pins. That's why in "no-tap" bowling, nine pins counts as a strike.

13   Except maybe when it comes to the solid 8-pin – that is truly an unlucky break!

14   We explained that the pocket is from the 16½ to the 18½ boards. ¾ pocket is the 17 board, which sometimes yields a 10-pin leave.

thin (as in the case of a ball that deflects too much) it will lay in the right gutter and not have enough impetus to pop out and topple the 10[15]. If it is cut too flush, it will jump up and around the 10-pin[16].

The most common question you hear among bowlers who carry between a 180 and a 220 average is, "How do I keep from leaving the 10-pin?" Honestly, from a lane play or an equipment standpoint, there are more possible adjustments you can try to combat leaving the 10-pin than there are lanes in your local bowling center. But what I've found is the best way is to throw your best shot more consistently. When a pro starts carrying that ¾ pocket hit by snapping the 10 out off the wall, that's when you're going to see him show the greatest amount of excitement. Why? Because a pro knows that when he's got the snap-10 shot working, he'll have a great chance to win that day. Anyone can carry a dead-flush pocket hit, but when you start to see that 10-pin snap out on a ¾ pocket hit, you know you are throwing it good that day!

Turning Bowling into a Simple Game

On the surface, bowling seems like such a simple game – throw a ball down a 60-foot lane and try to knock down as many pins as you can in the fewest number of attempts possible. But as the game evolved into a sport, and people began to value a person's ability to knock down pins with efficiency, complexities began to arise. Certain individuals developed techniques that proved more effective than others, and others tried to copy them or developed their own techniques that worked for them. Over time, many different styles claimed success and

---

15   This is called a "weak10 " or a "flat 10."

16   This is called a "solid 10" or "ringing 10."

then – BOOM! – technology is introduced into the equation, spawning still greater complexity. In bowling, the sport has certainly reached the point where the amount of information out there can certainly be overwhelming to a person who is simply trying to improve his scores. My advice to you is to simplify the process.

The history of the sport has proven that there is a wide range of styles that can enjoy success. All I've done is to find the links that these styles have in common that can be applied to any bowler's game to help him to improve. Understanding and applying my system is the first step in simplifying the sport so that it once again can be boiled down to it's essential elements, which are picking the best possible strategy for conquering a given lane, oil pattern and equipment combination that will unleash the greatest possible scoring potential in whatever competitive environment in which you choose to test yourself. Going in with a sound physical game is the first step toward clearing your mind and allowing yourself to focus on the next level of variables that the challenging sport of bowling is sure to throw at you. Heck, one day I may even decide to write a book on lane play or equipment strategy but, for now, I felt it was time for me to share my proven methods on the physical game with others so that you can get the most out of this great, lifelong sport that I've been lucky enough to enjoy for nearly my entire life.

Summing Up My Philosophy

There are only two types of people who walk through the doors of a bowling center: 1) Bowlers and 2) People who bowl. There's a big difference between the two. My job as a bowling instructor is to help retain bowlers and to convert "people who bowl" into "bowlers." The only way I know how to do that is to work with both categories of people to help make them better at bowling – because when you're getting better at something, you're not going to quit! The latest figures show that there are about 2 million people in the U.S. who are bowlers. These are the people who bowl in a sanctioned league each week. On the other hand, there are about 70 million people who bowl at least once a year. Converting those 70 million into league bowlers is a good thing for everyone in the bowling industry. More bowlers means more business for bowling centers, more business for pro shops and equipment manufacturers, and more people to watch professional bowling on TV. I believe the key to making the whole thing grow is to provide better coaching, and I truly hope that this book can help in that process.

As someone who spends his time devoted to the pursuit of helping bowlers to improve, I can honestly say that there is no greater reward than seeing the look on a person's face when he realizes he's getting better at something – in this case the sport of bowling. Since I developed my system and began devoting my career (and, really my life) to teaching it to bowlers, it is the happiest I've ever been – even more so than when I won on Tour against the greatest bowlers in the world. It's been the goal of this book to communicate my philosophy in a way that allows you to apply it to your own game in order to simplify what can sometimes be a rather complicated sport. And no matter what level of the sport you currently reside, I truly believe whole-heartedly that it is easily within your grasp to reach whatever goal you wish to attain in this great sport, so long as you are willing to apply yourself to the task. I wish you nothing but the best in your journey, and if there is ever anything more I can do to help you, I hope to be around for as long as I can, whether it's on the PBA Tour, at my camps and clinics or giving private lessons!

Case Study #6
The Invincible Bill O'Neill

When I first started working with Bill O'Neill a few years back, he was already one of the best up-and-coming young talents in the bowling world. He was a perennial first team All-American at Saginaw Valley State, and had worked his way into becoming one of the best young stars on the PBA Tour. But, being the kind of person who is never satisfied and continually wants to get better, he came to me asking if I could help him. After watching him throw shots for a while, I could see that really the only flaw in his game was that his right leg had a tendency to be all over the place during the release and the slide. After noticing this, I said to Bill, "Wow. I'll bet when the lanes start to hook a little bit and allow you to open up your angle[17], you really kill them. But you struggle when the lanes are fresh[18], really tight[19] or kind of tough[20]."

"Yeah! Exactly! How did you know?" said Bill.

17　Opening up your angle means throwing to the break point from further to the left. For example, if the break point is the 7th board at 40 feet and your laydown is the 20th board, then opening up your angle means moving your laydown left of the 20th board and using the same breakpoint at 40 feet.

18　Freshly oiled.

19　Refers to a high volume of oil or a low-friction lane surface, making it difficult for a bowler to hook the ball.

20　An oil pattern that is relatively flat, not allowing for much, if any, mistake area on the lane, best exemplified by the U.S. Open. Bill won the U.S. Open in 2010 after we started working together.

I explained to him about his back leg and how whenever it kicked up a little too high his shoulders would open up, which would in turn open up his swing path and project the ball too far to the right. On drier lanes, or when the lanes began to open up after a few games of lane play, those shots would recover and still hit the pocket (and more often than not, strike). But when there wasn't any room to the right, or the lanes required you to play a straighter line to the pocket, those shots resulted in washouts[21] or 2-10 leaves. I told Bill that if he could learn to control his back leg and keep it firing to a consistent spot time after time, his scores would go up on the fresh and he would still be a monster (actually, even more of a monster) when the lanes started hooking.

Boy was I right about that. In the 2009-2010 season Bill won his first PBA Tour title at the World Series of Bowling Chameleon Championship, then, a few weeks later, won his first major at the 2010 U.S. Open, bowling one of the best games (a 268 against Mike Scroggins) on one of the toughest oil patterns you'll ever see in the title match of a nationally-televised major championship. That year, Bill finished in a tie with two other bowlers in Player of the Year points (but was named runner-up to Walter Ray Williams Jr. due to the tie-breaker rule).

The following season, Bill continued his dominance, when he led the 60-game World Series of Bowling PBA World Championship qualifying over one of the best fields in PBA history. He ultimately lost the title to Chris Barnes in a great 267-237 title match, where both guys bowled near-flawless games (one of my proudest moments as a coach). But maybe the best performance I've seen from Bill yet was when he won the World

---

21 A combination leave where the headpin remains standing and the other remaining pins are separated by one or more rows of fallen pins. It's basically a split except we don't call it that because the headpin is still left standing.

Series of Bowling Viper Championship a few weeks before that. On that particular ESPN telecast, Bill mowed over four world-class opponents on an extremely tough oil pattern, bowling games of 244, 242 (with an open frame in the 10th because the game was wrapped up and he wanted to throw a "test" shot), 248 and 236. His opponents, meanwhile, averaged just 191 for the day, giving Bill an average margin of victory of over 50 pins a game! Needless to say, this is not a very common occurrence against the quality of competition you find out on the PBA Tour. And if you go back and watch that show, the thing you'll notice about Bill's game mechanically is just how steady he keeps that back leg on each and every shot. I mean, it just goes to the same place on an amazing 42 out of 44 shots!

Nowadays, whenever I work with Bill it's usually a situation where he comes to me with a problem, I watch him throw a few shots, we make a small change or two (usually, our sessions are between five and 25 minutes) and then he tells me, "OK, I'm good." Then he goes out and kicks some serious butt. There are even times when he'll come to me to see if there's anything I could suggest that he could improve upon. If I'm not seeing anything to fix I'll tell him, "Just be ready to bowl when it's your turn." The first time I told him that he said, "Huh? What does that mean."

I said, "That means you're throwing it great and anything I'd tell you would only mess it up – so just be ready to bowl when it's your turn." Sometimes as a coach, it's better to just keep your mouth shut and let your bowler go out and do his thing!

Acknowledgments

This project had many helping hands, and I'll do my best to thank them now.

First to Billy Hall, for getting me back into the game.

Jim and Eileen Martin, of Incline Village, NV. Your friendship I will never forget.

Gary Forman and Dave Osborn the owners of Fountain Bowl, my home center, and their amazing staff.

Ed Gallagher, and Ebonite International, thank you, my friend, for all you've done for me.

Linda and John Davis of Davis Bowling Supply, for helping create Camp Bakes, its all in the details!

To Linda Voorhees—all I can say is 'Thank You!!'

All my Camp Bakes coaches: John Gaines, Kendra Gaines, Robin Romeo, Kim Terrell-Kearney, Lynda Barnes, Chris Barnes, Joe Hutchinson, Doug Kent, Jason Couch, Dave Wodka, Tom Laskow, Dino Castillo, Chris Cecere, Barry Asher, Tommy Jones, and Dave Husted, you guys are the best!

To John Gaines for "seeing" it first, our phone conversations have been invaluable!

Jeff Crews, thanks for always being calm when I'm not!

Kevin Tomkins, for helping design the first Camp Bakes at the dining room table on Christmas eve. Its still working!

Jim Welch and Dennis Matthews and their staff at Strike Zone Sunset Station, home of Camp Bakes.

Chuck Gardner, for all of our conversations, you are the hardest-working man in bowling!

Ricky Corona, you're a great friend, and your attitude is an inspiration to me.

Thanks to my uncle, Don Baker, for the "engineer's" point of view, but more importantly, for being the best Uncle ever!

A huge "thank you" to Jason Thomas, for never getting discouraged, no matter how many times I made you change it! Thanks my friend!

To Tommy Jones, Chris Barnes, Jason Couch, Bill O'Neill, Mika Koivuniemi, and Michael Fagan, thank you for trusting me with your games, it's an honor to work with you guys!

To all the bowlers I have had the pleasure to coach, thank you!!

Barry Asher, the big brother I never had, thanks Star!

Chris Barnes, for knowing how to push me to get this project done. I know I will always get an honest opinion. I may not like it, but its always the truth – thank you my friend!

Dave Husted, you've been my best friend for over 30 years, not much else needs to be said – love you brother!

To my family, no matter if it was a baseball field, a basketball court, or a bowling center, and now coaching, you have always been there and supported me, I can't thank you enough, especially to my two sisters, Suzanne and Nicole, I love you.

My Mom, Patsy Bouvian, I know I can always count on you.

My two boys, Myles and Gage, you are my proudest achievement!

My Dad, J. Nick Baker, for never letting me live a life of quiet desperation.

Shannon, thanks for saving me, hope I saved you!

About the Author

Mark Baker has been active in the sport of bowling for more than 30 years, as a competitor, as a salesperson and, now, as an instructor.

Mark, a Southern California (Orange County) native, was an avid athlete, excelling in baseball and earning national recognition and accolades as an outstanding high school basketball player, in addition to establishing himself as one of Southern California's top junior bowlers ever.

Turning pro in 1982, Mark enjoyed a very successful bowling career, earning four PBA National Tour titles and appearing on television as a top-five finalist on more than two dozen occasions. In the mid 1980's he established himself as one of the premier players in the world, earning the "George Young High Average Award" in 1985 and a selection to the prestigious Bowlers Journal All-American First Team.

Mark's professional bowling career was shortened due to a serious back injury but his bowling exploits earned him inductions into both the Orange County and Southern California Bowling Halls of Fame.

While working as the Southern California Sales Manager

for Cal Bowling Supply, Mark expanded his coaching business, rapidly growing his private clientele and developing "Camp Bakes" – which is now considered one of the premier bowling camps in the world.

For his achievements in coaching, Mark has been named one of the "Top 100 Coaches in the United States" by Bowlers Journal International magazine on three separate occasions and he also coaches several of the top bowlers on the PBA Tour, including PBA Players of the Year Chris Barnes, Tommy Jones and Mika Koivuniemi, three-time PBA Tournament of Champions winner Jason Couch, 2009 U.S. Open Champion Bill O'Neill and 2012 USBC Masters Champion Mike Fagan.

Mark currently lives in Yorba Linda, California with his wife Shannon and son Gage.

CPSIA information can be obtained
at www.ICGtesting.com
Printed in the USA
BVOW09s0851120318
510167BV00002B/171/P